The Master Builder's
APPRENTICE

Revealing God's Supernatural Blueprint for Your Destiny

JANICE L. KRIEGER

ROSE A. HUNT

Bible quotations are taken from several Bible versions. The particular version is indicated by the following abbreviations.

AMP	Amplified® Bible. Copyright©1954, 1958, 1962, 1964, 1965, 1987 by Lockman Foundation.

KJV	*The King James Version*®. Thomas Nelson, Inc.

NKJV	*New King James Version*®. Copyright©1982 by Thomas Nelson, Inc.

NLT	*Holy Bible New Living Translation*. Copyright ©1996, 2004, 2007 by Tyndale House Publishers, Inc.

The Message. Copyright©1993, 1994, 1995, 1996, 2000, 2001, 2002 by Eugene Peterson, NavPress Publishing Group.

All rights reserved.

ISBN:	1479298565

ISBN 13:	9781479298563

Library of Congress Control Number: 2012916975
CreateSpace, Independent Publishing Platform.
North Charleston, South Carolina

TABLE OF CONTENTS

Acknowledgements		v
Foreword		vii
Introduction		ix
Chapter 1	Embrace Small Beginnings	1
Chapter 2	Establishing God's Throne in Our Heart	13
Chapter 3	Called to Unity	21
Chapter 4	The Anointing	35
Chapter 5	Establishing a Foundation	45
Chapter 6	God's Governmental Structure	61
Chapter 7	The Leader: Deliverer and Forerunner	71
Chapter 8	Fashioned by the Potter	85
Chapter 9	Building with God's Heart	99
Chapter 10	Nehemiah – Master Builder	111
Chapter 11	Charge and Change the Atmosphere	123
Chapter 12	Warfare Worship	135
Epilogue – Concepts in Practice		145
Glossary		163
Endnotes		171

ACKNOWLEDGEMENTS

We want to acknowledge the help and support we received from our *Glory Seekers* Bible study members in reviewing, editing and providing feedback on this manuscript, particularly Alex Lawlor and Kareemah El-Amin. Without your prayers, support and active participation, this book would not have been what God has called it to be—*a lamp to guide others in following God's blueprint of a supernatural work*. Thank you also to Rev. Karen Connell, *of Extended Life Christian Training Ministry* who reviewed the manuscript and gave solid biblical suggestions which have been incorporated into the text.

FOREWORD

PSALM 91:1

He that dwelleth in the secret place of the most High shall abide under the shadow of the Almighty.

What is destiny? *It is the pre-designed course God created for our life from the foundation of the world.* The only way we can find our destiny is if we seek his mind, heart and desires. If we acknowledge him in all our ways, HE WILL direct our path (Proverbs 3:6). If we do not diligently seek him on which path is our destiny, we will end up walking in the *shadow of what could be* and never experience the depth, the height nor the width—the essence of the fullness of God's plan for our life.

God says we can experience the fullness of our destiny (John 10:10 NKJV: *The thief does not come except to steal, and to kill, and to destroy. I have come that they may have life, and that they may have it more abundantly.*) Many believers have settled for a mere remnant of their destiny.

If we are to walk in our divine destiny, we must come under the *shadow of the Almighty*; as we move into this divine place of hiddenness and protection, God will *overshadow* us—this is the place of *conception*.

When God is birthing a work in us, we feel at odds with the process, but we can sense something significant is stirring within us. Perhaps, through prayer or a scripture passage, the Lord's voice awakens our spirit to the plan in his heart for our destiny. At this point, we must turn aside to see the burning bush—the fire his Spirit has ignited in our soul.

We begin seeking and pursuing this undefined prompting. God is knitting together inside of us a pattern of something supernatural that only he can do. As the natural birth process is fragile, so is the spiritual.

Gestation is the process of development from conception to birth of a fetus in the Mother's womb. Similarly, spiritual gestation is God maturing what he is knitting together in the womb of our spirit. What is born from this process is a supernatural work of God destined to leave *his footprint* not only in this world, but in the world to come.

Only when we walk in what was birthed under the shadow of the Almighty do we become an apprentice of the Master. In this position of intimacy, God reveals the supernatural blueprint to move us into our destiny — that place of rest where *He* accomplishes in and through us the divine purpose for which we were created. Otherwise, we journey in the shadow of what could be.

You are destined for the supernatural — embrace what is emerging within you. He has a plan for your life allow him to reveal it, and then pursue it.

INTRODUCTION

A supernatural work of God is one in which God is the author and builder of the framework. The concept, architecture and plans are the result of divine revelation. The work is not the result of human strategies, structures, and inspiration, rather the impartation of the Holy Spirit to a believer who is fully submitted to the Lordship of Jesus Christ. It is a place of humility and surrender of the mind, will and emotions to the plans and purposes of the Father.

For a supernatural work to succeed two elements are invariably present. First, it is founded upon unorthodox God-revealed strategies and tactics. For too long, it has been the practice of the body of Christ to duplicate a successful framework created in another part of the body and implement it as a "cookie-cutter" model. While initially the framework was God-breathed for a particular part of the body of Christ, we humans tend to begin to reason and rationalize the structure into something that is comfortable and amenable to people so that it can be adapted on a broad scale. At this juncture, it becomes yet another program or project without miraculous power to cause genuine transformation; it merely blesses at a superficial level. We've become so accustomed to operating at this level that few recognize that authentic change is not taking place.

Secondly, a supernatural work has at its core, a person or group willing to respond with radical obedience. Numerous references are recorded in the scriptures of God giving an unrealistic, unconventional strategy in response to a prayer for guidance or deliverance. For example, God gave Joshua an utterly improbable strategy to break through the walls at Jericho. The Lord instructed Joshua that the army was to walk around the city walls once a day followed by seven priests carrying the Ark and a trumpet. The priests were to continually blow the trumpets as they circled the city. On the seventh day, they marched around seven times; the priests blew the trumpets in one loud, long blast and the army shouted—AND THE WALLS FELL DOWN!

This must have appeared a preposterous battle plan to Joshua and his army. How could walking around the city and blowing horns collapse the walls? Jericho was one of the Israelites first battles to take the Promised Land; if they failed to capture Jericho, their credibility as a fighting force would be destroyed. The fear instilled in the people of the land at the recounting of the God of Israel's miracles, such as the parting of the Red Sea, would vanish. The Israelites would be obliterated as a people. Everything was at stake, yet Joshua responded with radical obedience to a plan that had no reasonable chance of success, except that it was God's plan. They obeyed instantly and completely, and the rest is history.

If you are seeking a supernatural work of God, one that demonstrates the miraculous power of God and creates genuine transformation, you must earnestly seek God and purpose in your heart to unconditionally submit to his ways, his thoughts and his purposes. In this place of humble submission he will test how you respond; whether you will obey him or not. God seeks three demonstrations of our commitment. 1) Obey his Commands—follow exactly the revelation of the framework/foundation; 2) Walk in his Ways—structure exactly according to his pattern, protocol and timing; and 3) Fear him—revere him and seek to please him rather than falling prey to the *fear of man*. If we **do** (not just plan or intend) these fundamentals, nothing will be lacking to accomplish the work. The heavens will be opened to us, and his storehouse of resources will overflow into our account.

The incident of Balaam's donkey recorded in the book of Numbers 22 and 23, demonstrates that it is impossible for man to curse what God has blessed, as long as the believer(s) stay in alignment with his Word. King Balak of Moab sent messengers to the Lord's prophet Balaam, with money in hand, to urge him to curse the Israelites whom the king feared would infiltrate his country. However, when Balaam prayed to the Lord, God said not to curse the Israelites for he had blessed them. Despite Balaam's refusal to curse Israel, the messengers returned again. Balaam inquired of the Lord a second time. The Lord told Balaam to go with the men to the mountain, but only prophesy what the he told him. Nevertheless, when Balaam saddled his donkey and left with the King and his messengers, the Lord was displeased with his eager attitude, and

Introduction

sent an angel to stand in the road to kill him. The donkey saw the angel and refused to move forward. In a fit of temper, Balaam struck the donkey repeatedly with his staff. Then the Lord caused the donkey to speak; the Lord opened Balaam's eyes and he saw the angel in the road with a drawn sword. Still, the Lord told him to continue to the mountain; however, he was only to say the words the Lord would give him. On the mountain top, again he blessed Israel and King Balak was livid. What God had blessed, Balaam was unable to curse.

When we operate out of a God-revealed framework, the Lord sends his angels to protect, minister to us, and war over us (Daniel 10:13). Our God enters into covenant with us as he did with the Israelites (Exodus 34:10, 14). He promises to do the miraculous, displaying his power and glory *if* we will not compromise the plan or the purpose to appease people.

If you believe God is calling you to a supernatural work— begin to pursue it without delay. Commit to completing the work, being faithful in your actions, trusting God without wavering, and expecting the absolute best of everything you express, demonstrate and proclaim in the name of Jesus. Congratulations! Go forth as a mighty and powerful vessel of God. You are destined to help establish his Kingdom on earth. Read on—this book is for you!

Chapter 1

EMBRACE SMALL BEGINNINGS

The thought of starting a supernatural work is daunting to our natural mind. It overwhelms our emotions. At this juncture, many believers begin to plan and reason, or intellectualize what God has stirred in their hearts. We look about us to circumstances that are unfavorable, to our lack of expertise, connections, or material resources to make what God has spoken a reality and conclude it's impossible. This is exactly the place God desires as we have moved from the position of *"doing it in our own strength"* to relying on God's ability to make it happen.

As simplistic as it may sound, the place to start a supernatural work of God is *where you are*! God always starts with an individual whose heart is turned toward him. A man or woman who is listening to what the Spirit is saying—Abraham, Moses, Joshua, Samuel, Ruth, David, Esther, Abigail, Zerubbabel, Paul, and John are a few biblical examples.

Let us look in particular at Zerubbabel. Zerubbabel was born in Babylon during the captivity of Judah. He was the grandson of Jeconiah (Jehoiakim), the king of Judah when the nation was taken captive. After 70 years of captivity, King Cyrus made a proclamation that a small contingent of exiled Jews could return to their homeland. Zerubbabel returned as the highest ranking governmental leader, and Joshua, the High Priest, as the highest ranking religious leader. Together they ruled the Jews in Jerusalem. Their objective in returning was to rebuild the temple.

Upon their arrival in Jerusalem, the exiled Jews found the conditions appalling. The surrounding land was but rubble and the temple in ruin. The inhabitants lived in wretched poverty and had intermarried with the neighboring people. All the nations encircling them were hostile and bitterly opposed to the small band of Jews rebuilding their temple.

Zerubbabel, though a descendant of a king, was disqualified in the people's eyes because the prophet Jeremiah had decreed a curse from God on Zerubbabel's grandfather that denied his descendants a kingly blessing and rule.

> *"As surely as I live," says the LORD, "I will abandon you, Jehoiachin son of Jehoiakim, king of Judah. Even if you were the signet ring on my hand, I would pull you off....Let the record show that this man Jehoiachin was childless. He is a failure, for none of his children will succeed him on the throne of David to rule over Judah" (Jeremiah 22:24 & 30 NLT).*

The circumstances were highly unfavorable at best. Despite the deplorable conditions, Zerubbabel led the people in re-laying the foundations of the temple and rebuilding the altar of sacrifice. The reconstruction incited the enemies of Judah. They badgered, taunted and attacked the Jews repeatedly. Finally the work was stopped for 16 years after their enemies wrote a letter to the new king Xerxes falsely accusing the Jews of rebuilding the temple in rebellion to the king.

Through the prophets Haggai and Zechariah, the Lord speaks to Zerubbabel about the reconstruction of the Temple, though its start is miniscule, it is a supernatural work. Additionally, the Lord informs him that He has reversed the curse, anointing Zerubbabel with His divine authority.

> *Then another message came to me from the LORD: "Zerubbabel is the one who laid the foundation of this Temple, and he will complete it. Then you will know that the LORD of Heavens Armies has sent me. Do not despise*

these small beginnings, for the LORD rejoices to see the work begin, to see the plumb line in Zerubbabel's hand. (The seven eyes represent the eyes of the LORD that search all around the world.)" (Zechariah 4:8-10 NLT).

...I will honor you Zerubbabel son of Shealtiel, my servant. I will make you like a signet ring on my finger, says the Lord, for I have chosen you. I, the LORD of Heaven's Armies, have spoken!" (Haggai 2:23 NLT).

A signet ring[1] was a unique ring worn by a person of wealth or in a position of influence. It held the personal seal of its owner rather than a jewel. When the owner wanted to prove that he or she was the originator of a document, he or she melted some wax on the document to seal it and pressed his/her signet ring into the wax. The impression left by the signet ring was proof that the letter was authentic. A signet ring was a stamp of approval that sealed a proclamation, decree or law so that it could not be broken, undone or reversed.

By calling Zerubbabel his signet ring, God was decreeing that Zerubbabel would be his proof of authenticity. Through Zerubbabel, God's promises would be fulfilled, proving that his word was true (authentic). The work was his—a supernatural work and Zerubbabel the chosen vessel to carry it out.

Interestingly, Zerubbabel's name[2] is a combination of two Hebrew words—*zarab* to flow away. In the King James Version of the Bible, *zarab* is translated "warm wax." The second Hebrew word is *babel* meaning confusion by mixing. Again in the King James Version, this word is translated as Babel or Babylon.

On a spiritual level, the Lord decreed Zerubbabel as his signet ring. The melting of Zerubbabel's life took him from confusion to transformation. A transformation process that changed him into a truly humble and obedient servant, combined with the Lord's promised authority—the anointing (signet ring), rebuilt what had fallen. In essence, the decree was the foundation. It could not be broken or undone. It was sealed with the wax of the anointing; and therefore, set up and established with the King's (God's) power and authority of decree to rebuild that which has fallen.

Zerubbabel's life speaks of God's undeserved grace and favor. He is an illustration of a believer who started with a deficit, just like many of us, whether it was the result of our own poor choices, or we were "born into it" like Zerubbabel. Poor choices, a curse, or any other obstacle or hindrance will not disqualify you from becoming a chosen instrument to carry out a supernatural work of God! As the Apostle Paul so aptly penned, *"And I am convinced that nothing can ever separate us from God's love. Neither death nor life, neither angels nor demons, neither our fears for today nor our worries about tomorrow – not even the powers of hell can separate us from God's love. No power in the sky above or in the earth below – indeed, noting in all creation will ever be able to separate us from the love of God that is revealed in Christ Jesus our Lord"* (Romans 8:38-39 NLT).

If we surrender our life to the Lord Jesus Christ and press on toward the mark of the high calling of Christ, we will do as Paul declares in Phil. 3: 13-14 NLT *"...I focus on this one thing: Forgetting the past and looking forward to what lies ahead, I press on to reach the end of the race and receive the heavenly prize for which God, thorough Christ Jesus is calling us."*

God loves us and desires to show his compassion and mercy toward us. He wants to demonstrate his glory through your life. The past is *under the blood of Christ* and will not disqualify you from his *Hall of Overcomers*. If you, with Zerubbabel-like determination and commitment, capture God's heart of what he is doing in the earth, he will reveal his kingdom plan and purpose to you in a supernatural work. This work will take you beyond your natural comprehension and abilities in order to fulfill it. Zerubbabel's humility and obedience changed God's heart and put him back into alignment with the Word of God, and in right standing to be in the hall of fame of the ancestry of the Messiah. *"...Shealtiel was the father of Zerubbabel. Zerubbabel was the father of Abiud..."* (Matthew 1:13 NLT).

PERSONAL TRANSFORMATION PROCESS

To lead a supernatural work of God, we must function in both the Kingly (Zerubbabel) and Priestly (Joshua) roles as described in the book of Zechariah. The supernatural requires transformation. Our natural thoughts, abilities and ways of doing things are at enmity with God. The scripture is very clear on this point.

For they that are after the flesh do mind the things of the flesh; but they that are after the Spirit the things of the Spirit. For to be carnally minded is death; but to be spiritually minded is life and peace. So then they that are in the flesh cannot please God (Romans 8:5-8 KJV).

We find this disconcerting because we have been conditioned from birth to function according to the physical world around us. We have spent our lives operating in the physical dimension, it is normal and natural to us—it breeds comfortability. However, our comfort zone is a *death* zone hostile to a supernatural work of God. The Lord instructs Zerubbabel that the work cannot be accomplished through an arm of flesh.

Then he said to me, "This is what the LORD says to Zerubbabel: It is not by force nor by strength but by my Spirit says the LORD of Heaven's Armies. Nothing, not even a mighty mountain will stand in Zerubbabel's way; it will become a level plain before him! And when Zerubbabel sets the final stone of the Temple in place, the people will shout: 'may God bless it! May God bless it'" (Zechariah 4:6-7 NLT).

Comfort breeds complacency and dependency on our own abilities, and on systems and structures that are already in place. This is a subtle strategy of the enemy to keep us in bondage to the world in which he has access to control, thwart and dominate the work. For example, the enemy seeks to create a hierarchical framework. A hierarchy is based on levels of control, with those closest to the top of the pyramid exercising the most power. While this model may be practical in carrying out programs and projects, it is not a divine structure—it is a corporate structure patterned after the world, which is under Satan's control.

The Scriptures reveal that a hierarchy breeds corruption. *Don't be surprised if you see a poor person being oppressed by the powerful and if justice is being miscarried throughout the land. For every official is under orders from higher up, and matters of justice get lost in red tape and bureaucracy* (Ecclesiastes 5:8 NLT). If we build according to Satan's framework, we are giving him legal access to infiltrate it. Then the church wonders why it has no "power" and we do not see the manifestation of the miraculous. Simply put, God is not in it!

Filthy Garments

Like Joshua, the High Priest, before God does a supernatural work through us, he does a supernatural work in us. First, our filthy garments must be removed.

> *Now Joshua was clothed with filthy garments and stood before the angel. And he answered and spake unto to those that stood before him saying, Take away the filthy garments from him. And unto him he said, Behold, I have caused thine iniquity to pass from thee, and I will clothe thee with change of raiment (Zechariah 3:3-4 KJV).*

What are our filthy garments? They represent our flesh nature that consists of how our mind and behaviors have been conditioned as we operate in demonic structures and filter our beliefs through our cultural mindsets. Filthy garments symbolize man's way of being and doing things.

Personal transformation occurs when we take off the filth of the world (thinking as the world thinks and behaving in accordance with our cultural norms), and put on Christ. This is an action empowered by the Holy Spirit. It is not something we can do in our strength. We must make a conscious decision to submit and surrender to this renewing and purification process of the Holy Spirit within us.

Putting on Christ consists of many elements: 1) renewing our mind; 2) overcoming evil with good; 3) cultivating a Godly character built upon the fruit of the Spirit; 4) becoming a fruitful vine intimately attached to the root that multiplies and produces good fruit for the Kingdom; and 5) walking in faith. This is not an exhaustive list of all the fundamentals, but pivotal elements to activating a supernatural work of God. Three of the elements—renewing our mind, cultivating an intimate relationship and walking in faith—are the *inner* garments of putting on Christ.

Renewing our Mind

The primary avenue to renewing the mind is through washing it with the Word of God. The scripture says we are made *holy and clean, washed by the cleansing of God's word* (Eph. 5:26 NLT). Our natural minds have been structured according to a fallen world. This structure reinforces self-will, reason, ambition and power. Unless we instill God's Word into our heart, our mind will be in continual dissonance with our Spirit. We will be what the Bible calls double-minded.

Unless our thoughts are permeated with scripture, our spirit man responds to what the Lord is speaking to us, but our mind begins to fight against it. If our thought patterns are not founded on the Word, we will begin to reason, doubt or waver on what the Lord is speaking into our heart. Our faith lies in our Spirit, not in our mind. The New Living Translation expresses this dissonance of double-mindedness beautifully.

> *If you need wisdom, ask our generous God, and he will give it to you. He will not rebuke you for asking. But when you ask him, be sure that your faith is in God alone. Do not waver, for a person with a divided loyalty is as unsettled as a wave of the sea that is blown and tossed by the wind. Such people should not expect to receive anything from the Lord. Their loyalty is divided between God and the world, and they are unstable in everything they do (James 1:5-8 NLT).*

A renewed mind means our belief system, from which our thoughts flow, is accessing the database of the Word of God and standing in faith on that alone to process and filter all information coming into the mind. Without a renewed mind, we will waver in double-mindedness. Our spirit is standing in faith but our mind is not in submission to the Word of God; rather, it is accessing the database of the world—our cultural beliefs and mindsets. In this state, our mind cannot come into agreement with our faith. Therefore, we become double-minded; our fleshly mind wavers crossing over into unbelief while our spirit is standing in Truth. Hence, the Lord can do nothing for us as *"...a house divided against itself, that house cannot stand"* (Mark 3:25 KJV). This Scripture states Satan cannot cast out Satan (v. 23). If we believe his lies and come into agreement with him in our mind, we become unstable; our loyalties are divided between the world and the Spirit.

Unfortunately, it is from this place of double-mindedness that most of the works of the body of Christ originate. God quickens our spirit and speaks a supernatural work into our heart. We receive the word in our Spirit, but then begin to construct the framework with our mind following the thought patterns of the world, and placing the work within the structures built by the world. As illustration, God speaks into our spirit to build a global prayer network. Instead of allowing the Lord to direct and form the structure, immediately an unrenewed mind will look to the technology of the world to construct it, rather than to wait on God to reveal the framework. At this point, the mind will be in dissonance to the Spirit; a man-made structure will result, not an anointed, supernatural work of God. Disturbingly, most believers in the body of Christ can no longer distinguish between the two.

As we study and meditate upon Scripture, we must ensure that we are not "cherry picking" verses that align with our own preferences and desires. Instead, we seek out the whole counsel of God on a particular subject within the context in which it was written in the Scripture. A helpful tool to discern whether we are cherry picking, or truly accessing God's full counsel, is to put what we extract to a simple test. Any *content* we have extracted from the scripture must be in alignment with the *context* from which it was taken; otherwise, we are founding it on a *false premise*. A false premise can never lead us to Truth.

Pastor and author Karen Connell, in her booklet *Normalizing Evil*[3] demonstrates the dangers of taking scripture content out of biblical context. Connell states, "All false doctrines are based upon either no Scriptural proof or Scriptures being taken out of their context in order to support false ideas." She illustrates this point through the oft quoted scripture of Luke 6:38 NKJV, *Give, and it will be given to you: good measure, pressed down, shaken together, and running over will be put into your bosom. For with the measure that you use, it will be measured back to you.* Many teachers, pastors and evangelists take this scripture out of its context and claim that the more "seed" (money) you sow, the more money you will get in return from the Lord. If you give a minute amount, you will receive likewise, a small amount in return; or if you give a huge sum, you will get a huge amount back. Luke 6:38 is actually referring "to the "giving" and "receiving" of *condemnation* or *forgiveness* according to the measure we use to mete these out. The context has nothing to do with giving and receiving money!"

We have become quite lax in the body of Christ, taking verses out of their Scriptural context to support outside sources, our own ideas, desires or motives, rather than starting from the premise stated in the Scripture and building our beliefs on that foundation. No other foundation can be laid than that of the apostles and prophets with Jesus as the Chief Cornerstone. Ephesians 2:20 (NLT) Together, we *are his house, built on the foundation of the apostles and the prophets. And the cornerstone is Christ Jesus himself.* We must start with the premise in the Bible, not use a premise from an outside source, such as mythology, science, the occult, or our own ideas and desires. This is huge because false premises produce strongholds. In other words, we have given place to the enemy to construct a demonic structure in our mind that will hold us in bondage and blind us from seeing a Truth from God's perspective

The Bible clearly states if you start with a foolish premise your conclusion will be sheer madness! Ecclesiastes 10:12-13 (Living Bible) *It is pleasant listen to wise words, but a fool's speech brings him to ruin. Since he begins with a foolish premise, his conclusion is sheer madness. A fool knows all about the future and tells everyone in detail! But who can really know what is going to happen?* According to the scriptures, the world's wisdom is foolishness to God. 1 Corinthians 3:19 (NLT) *For the wisdom of this world is foolishness to God. As the Scriptures say, "He traps the wise in the snare of their own cleverness.* As Satan is the god of this world, this wisdom is demonically inspired and leads to death not life.

Intimate Relationship

While knowledge of God is paramount to renewing our mind, our relationship with God must go deeper. We must also experience God. Much of the superficiality in the body of Christ is the result of head knowledge at the expense of heart knowledge. I can know about marriage informationally by reading various marriage manuals on the "how to's", until I believe I know the subject of marriage thoroughly. However, it is not until I am united in marriage and intimately acquainted with my spouse, that I *experience* marriage. It is at this point, I experience the "fullness" of a marriage relationship. So it is with our relationship with God. I can know all about him, but until I experience intimate moments in his presence, I do not know him in his fullness. This is a life-long quest.

We get to know our marriage partner through spending time with him or her, listening to what is on our spouse's heart—to what makes them happy and what grieves them. This is how we get to know God—it is called prayer and worship.

Cultivating an intimate relationship, lays the foundation for God to form you into a vessel through which he can execute a supernatural work. It is only through extended periods of time in his presence, not petitioning, but simply fellowshipping with him, that he begins to reveal the secrets of his heart to us. We begin to perceive aspects of his character—passionate love, unwavering faithfulness and stability, and his trustworthiness. Not only are we beginning to understand who he is and building an unshakeable trust, he is forming in us a vessel he can trust.

There is no short-cut to experiencing God; it requires time—extended periods of worship and basking in his presence. Worship increases our ability "to see" into the spiritual realm. Worship suspends our mind which keeps us time-bound to the earth, and releases our spirit into the eternal realm that is timeless—where everything is NOW. We access this realm by faith.

Walking in Faith

To walk in faith, we must be Spirit-led. We can only be Spirit-led if we are in constant communion with the Godhead through intimate fellowship. We cannot walk in faith with our mind in control. Our mind must be submitted to, and under the control of, the Holy Spirit. Faith is our *eyes to see* into the unseen world (the spiritual/heavenly realm). Through my eyes of faith, I am seated in the heavenly realm and I am able to walk in the Lord's presence as I live on earth—*For he raised us from the dead along with Christ and seated us with him in the heavenly realms because we are united with Christ Jesus* (Ephesians 2:6 NLT). I have access to the throne room of God—*Because of Christ and our faith in him, we can now come boldly and confidently into God's presence* (Ephesians 3:12 NLT).

The reason we have access to the throne room of God, by faith, is that faith is the *substance* that furnishes the way for us to "see" back to the place where we originated—in the eternal realm of God. We are eternal beings in an earthly body. We came from eternity and we will return there. This concept is further developed by Renny Mc Clean in his book *Eternity Invading Time*[4].

Hebrews 11:1 KJV declares: *Faith is the substance of things hoped for the evidence of things not seen*. In other words, faith that is real faith is *substance*. According to the online Encarta Dictionary, a definition of *substance*[5] is: tangible physical matter; a physical reality that can be touched and felt. Real faith is also *evidence*. Again, according to the online Encarta

Dictionary, a definition of *evidence*[6] is: a sign or proof; something that gives a sign or proof of the existence or truth of something, or that helps somebody come to a particular conclusion.

With these definitions in view, faith is tangible, a physical reality of the hope that can be touched and felt. It is a sign or proof of the existence, the truth of what is invisible. Consequently, *to walk in faith means to walk in the invisible and make it tangible*. How do we accomplish this?

Mary, Jesus' mother, provides an illustration of walking in faith. At the marriage feast in Cana, the wine had run out, an extreme embarrassment in that culture. Mary informs her son of the dilemma but Jesus responds that his hour—his time to perform miracles has not yet arrived. Despite this fact, Mary exercises her faith (*saying* to the servants "*Do whatever he tells you*," John 2:5 NLT). She places a demand on Jesus' anointing for miracles, pulling the manifestation from eternity. There is no time in eternity—everything is NOW!

The Father responds to her faith; the miracle is *released* in heaven. Jesus, who is our model of walking in the physical while being seated spiritually in the heavens, saw (with his eyes of faith) what the Father was doing and manifested the wine in the physical world. By Jesus' admission, "*I tell you the truth, the Son can do nothing by himself. He does only what he sees the Father doing. Whatever the Father does, the Son also does*" (John 5:19 NLT).

What does this all mean for us? Our faith is our *key card* to access the spiritual realm. With our *eyes* of faith we see into the invisible realm what God is doing—so that we can *declare* it. When we speak it out, it becomes *framed* in the spirit realm—it has *substance* (our faith is being mixed with the Spirit of God). It is no longer void, but can be *manifested*—visible *evidence* on the earth. God's word cannot return void; it will accomplish the purpose for which it was sent—*So shall my word be that goeth forth out of my mouth: it shall not return unto me void, but it shall accomplish that which I please, and it shall prosper in the thing whereto I sent it* (Isaiah 55:11 KJV).

To walk in faith requires two spiritual senses—hearing and seeing. We must be able to *hear* the voice of God (the Holy Spirit) before we can *see* with our eyes of faith what he is doing. The apostle Paul received both in his conversion experience on the road to Damascus. *He fell to the ground and heard a voice saying to him, "Saul! Saul! Why are you persecuting me?"* (Acts 9:4 NLT). Paul, called Saul at the time of his conversion, heard the voice of God. The intense light of the Lord's presence temporarily blinded Paul. In order for Paul to begin to see with eyes of faith, the scales had to be removed from his eyes—the physical blindness was symbolic of his spiritual blindness. *So Ananias went and found Saul. He laid his hands on him and said, "Brother Saul, the Lord Jesus who appeared to you on the road, has sent me so that you might regain your sight and be filled with the Holy Spirit" Instantly something like scales fell from Saul's eyes, and he regained his sight* (Acts 9:17-18 NLT). What Saul received was his ***measure of faith***—his spiritual eyes (Romans 12:3 KJV). From this moment on Paul "saw" the unseen world. It is available to us all.

The scripture declares, *But whenever someone turns to the Lord, the veil is taken away. For the Lord is the Sprit, and wherever the Lord is, there is freedom. So all of us who have had that veil removed* ***can see and reflect the glory of the Lord.*** *And the Lord—who is Spirit—makes us more and more like him as we are changed into his glorious image* (2 Cor. 3:16-18 NLT, emphasis added).

In the natural, we cannot call forth those things we can't see. However, with our eyes of faith functioning, we call those things that are not as though they are (Romans 4:17). We begin to call forth out of eternity the manifestation—out of the invisible the tangible comes forth. *This happened because Abraham believed in the God who brings the dead back to life and creates new things out of nothing* (Romans 4:17 NLT). . . . *Even God who quickeneth the dead, and calleth those things which be not as though they were* (Romans 4:17 KJV).

Pistis[7] the Greek word for **faith** used in the following scripture means: *reliance on and constancy in profession upon the Truth (Christ). That your faith should not stand in the wisdom of man but the power of God* (I Cor. 2:5 KJV). When we are in intimate fellowship with the Lord, our mind is submitted to, and controlled by, the Spirit. Our eyes of faith will be fully functioning; then we will confidently walk in faith. The power of God will be demonstrated in the work he has called us to—a supernatural work accompanied by resurrection power! You must call forth, and step into, what God is showing you and it will happen!

With our inner garments in place—the renewal of our mind, pursuing an intimate relationship with our creator, and walking in faith for the supernatural, we are ready to put on our outer garment, our robe of righteousness.

Chapter 2

ESTABLISHING GOD'S THRONE IN OUR HEART

A supernatural work requires a *genuine* believer. A genuine believer is a *separated* person—separated in the sense that the driving desire of the heart is to pursue holiness. A holy God can only dwell in a pure vessel. If God is going to do a supernatural work through us, he must establish his throne in our heart. Every believer must ask this question, "Who is on the throne in my heart?" Is it money, drugs, my children or my spouse? Or, is Jesus still my first love? Is he above and more important than anything else in my life including my job and my own desires? If Jesus is not first and central in your heart, he is not on the throne. Clarify this now. If something or someone is taking up the majority of your time and attention, it is an idol—no matter what or who it is. Rectify this situation now. Repent of putting Jesus in a lower position and ask him to take his rightful seat on the throne of your heart. After you have done so, you are ready to be clothed in the garment of righteousness.

In the previous chapter, we learned how we remove our filthy garments—our cultural, worldly mindsets, the belief systems of the world, and walking by our own abilities. We take them off by *putting on Christ*—starting with the *inner* garments of a renewed mind, intimate relationship with our Lord, and walking by faith. In this chapter we put on our *outer* garment—our robe of righteousness.

What is our robe of righteousness? First, it is enacting our *position* in Christ. We are righteous before God because of his Son, Jesus Christ— his shed blood upon the cross has paid the penalty for our sin. *For God in all his fullness was pleased to live in Christ, and through him God reconciled everything to himself. He made peace with everything in heaven and on earth by means of Christ's blood on the cross* (Colossians 1:19-20 NLT).

Jesus' death on the cross reconciled us back to the triune God; it has restored us to a place of peace—*right-alignment* with everything on earth AND heaven. Our righteousness in Christ achieved both purposes of God's eternal plan—reconciliation and restoration. We are now in a position of *oneness* with the Godhead and the heavenly realm; and restored to our rightful authority of dominion in the earth. Our oneness (unity) in the spiritual realm has seated us in heavenly places with Christ Jesus. *And hath raised us up together, and made us sit together in heavenly places in Christ Jesus* (Ephesians 2:6 KJV). From our heavenly location, we have access to God's throne. Here God reveals heavenly strategy—the purposes of his heart for the divine work he has called us to perform.

In the earthly realm, we are in *right*-alignment with all things. Unlike the spiritual realm, in which we come into unity with the Godhead and the heavenly realm, there are things on or in the earth, such as demonic forces, which we, as righteous vessels, cannot come into agreement. Our right-alignment with the things of earth and heaven gives us the *authority* to respond to situations in a righteous manner. We may have to speak a judgment of rebuke by our authority. That is why we are admonished to acknowledge him in all that we do, in order for him to direct our steps, our path, and our assignment.

Because Christ's death also restored our original dominion in the earth, we can exercise our authority in Christ to bring earth into alignment with heavenly purposes. *And God said let us make man in our image, after our likeness: and let them have dominion over the fish of the sea, and over the fowl of the air, and over the cattle, and over all the earth, and over every creeping thing that creepeth upon the earth* (Genesis 1:26 KJV). God's original intention was that we have authority over *all* things on the earth as part of our inheritance. Christ's death repurchased the land that was deeded to us at creation and our authority to rule over it.

Satan is an interloper; a thief who came to rob, kill and destroy (John 10:1). He exercises authority over, and thwarts the work God calls us to accomplish in the earth, *only* because believers do not exercise their rightful authority to destroy the works of the devil (I John 3:8). Satan is our adversary not our lord! The only authority he wields is that which we concede to him. We are exhorted in the Scriptures (KJV): *"neither give place to the devil"* (Eph. 4:27); *"to stand against the wiles of the devil"* (Eph. 6:11) and to be recovered *"out of the snare of the devil"* (2 Tim. 2:26).

Satan's primary weapon against believers is *deception*. He has deceived believers into thinking he is in control of the earth and we are powerless against his authority. His primary tools of deception are *wiles* — trickery, scams, hoaxes and charismatic appeals that mesmerize and captivate. Through the use of these tools he creates *snares* — traps that enslave believers in the world system which has been ensnared, and therefore, subject to his control. Consequently, we are commanded not to give *place* — position ourselves, identify with, or come under his authority by abdicating our authority in Christ and falling prey to the deceptions of the devil.

We are called to bring earth into alignment with heaven's purposes to achieve a supernatural work of God. The devil cannot destroy a supernatural work of God, as it is birthed in and through his life-giving power. The only means of destruction is if we, as believers, abort it by becoming ensnared by the wiles of the devil.

Our position in Christ has qualified us to put on our robe of righteousness; however, humility will determine whether we wear it.

GOD'S THRONE IN OUR HEART

Psalm 97:2 (KJV) declares that *"righteousness and justice are the habitation of his throne."* This verse signifies that righteousness and justice are the foundation of God's throne. If God is to establish his throne in our heart, it will be founded on righteousness and justice.

Isaiah prophesied that *"Zion will be restored by justice; those who repent will be revived by righteousness"* (Isaiah 1:27 NLT). What God spoke through Isaiah was that Jerusalem would not be his dwelling place again until *his throne* was established in her midst. Those in whom God's throne is established, love justice and walk in righteousness. They have a balanced perspective of God's love and His holiness. God's love exudes mercy, while his holiness requires judgment of all that offends it.

Many in the body of Christ have such an unbalanced view of God's love that they sincerely believe that God *only* extends mercy and never judgment. This perspective is unbiblical and totally offensive to the holiness of God. God is love, which means that his love is perfectly aligned with his throne. His love executes justice that is righteous to preserve his holiness.

God establishes his throne in our heart when we love justice—when we appropriate God's love through the lens of his holiness; then we will treat others fairly and with respect, regardless of race or position. Justice will be upheld in our heart as we walk in righteousness.

Righteousness guards justice. To wear our robe of righteousness, we must be re-clothed in a spirit of humility. This is the position from which we clothe ourselves in love so that we begin to see the bond of unity that produces the anointing. Micah 6:8 (NKJV) illustrates these concepts. *He has shown you, O man, what is good; And what does the LORD require of you but to do justly, to love mercy, and to walk humbly with your God?*

Humility

Many visualize a *robe of righteousness* as a beautiful, ornate robe of richly embroidered fabric. This is a misconception. A robe of righteousness is one whose beauty is not outwardly visible to the human eye; rather its beauty is woven into the fabric of a life controlled by a spirit of humility.

In our "religious" culture permeated by self-promotion, ambition, and desire for preeminence, true *humility* is loathed as a weakness found in those unsophisticated and unlearned in the Kingdom. We have exchanged the biblical meaning of humility *obeying the will of God regardless of its personal cost*[1] to pious platitudes: *"Let's not be critical"; "We don't want to offend anyone;" "I just want to love everyone."* Those adhering to this type of false humility always have a "nice" or "sympathetic" word which they construe as promoting *unity* in the church. However, when circumstances demand they stand up against error or take an unpopular stance, they disappear into the woodwork, unwilling to jeopardize their position or tarnish their reputation in the eyes of man.

However, if we look to biblical examples of humility, we find God's perspective. The ultimate example is Jesus.

Though he was God, he did not think of equality with God as something to cling to. Instead, he gave up his divine privileges; he took the humble position of a slave and was born as a human being. When he appeared in human form, he humbled himself in obedience to God and died a criminal's death on the cross (Philippians 2:6-8 NLT).

Jesus is our model of humility. He obeyed the will of God *to the point of death*. He did not use his divine privilege; rather he abdicated his position willing to suffer humiliation, loss of reputation, misunderstanding and persecution so that the purposes of God would be fulfilled through his life.

Humility is not founded on what men think of you. *It is founded on what God thinks of you*. Humility is not based on man's opinions or self-serving attitudes. To be humble does not mean to never offend. John the Baptist whom Jesus identified as the greatest prophet (Luke 7:28) lost his head because he spoke the truth which offended King Herod and his wife. No doubt the Pharisees celebrated John's demise as he had offended most of them too. Nevertheless, John stood for what was right—Herod had married his brother Philip's wife, an unlawful act (Mark 6:17). God called John to confront Herod, his obedience cost him his life.

Paul too endured trials, hardships, suffering and persecution because of his humility. He made enemies (Acts 21:27-30). Just the sight of Paul in the Temple in Jerusalem incited the Jews to rouse a mob to beat him with the intent to kill him. He offended the Jews by preaching Jesus as the Messiah (Acts 22:6-22). He offended the Christians by extending salvation to the gentiles without the Jewish requirement of circumcision (Acts 15:1-19). Paul confronted the Corinthian church for dishonoring the Lord's Supper (I Cor. 11:17-20). He also confronted them exposing the immorality among members, with one so bold as to be sleeping with his step-mother (I Cor. 5:1-5). Was Paul humble? Of course, the spirit of humility controlled Paul's actions and reactions.

Humility requires real courage. Again, let's look at Jesus. Jesus was direct. *"Woe unto you scribes and Pharisees, hypocrites! For ye make clean the outside of the cup and of the platter, but within they are full of extortion and excess"* (Matthew 23:25 KJV). Jesus didn't mince words with those that possessed the head knowledge, but their hearts were far from the Kingdom. Jesus identified the root of the problem and addressed it forthrightly.

In Luke Chapter 18, a rich young ruler approached Jesus and inquired what he needed to do to inherit eternal life. Jesus responded that he must keep the commandments, to which the man verified he had done from his youth. Jesus then got right to the point, *When Jesus heard his answer, he said, "There is still one thing you haven't done. Sell all your possessions and give the money to the poor, and you will have treasure in heaven. Then come, follow me"* (Luke 18:22 NLT).

Jesus pressed to the heart issue. The young man's heart did not belong to God even though he outwardly adhered to God's teachings; his idol was his money. He walked away; Jesus did not stop him; rather he revealed what was truly hindering him from entering the kingdom, and let him choose whom he would serve.

Jesus was *assertive, uncompromising and bold*. He confronted the moneychangers in the temple. In righteous anger, he overturned their tables and drove them out condemning their misuse of God's house—turning it from a house of prayer to a den of thieves (Matthew 21:12-13). Jesus acted from the Throne—righteousness and justice permeated his actions, demonstrating that hypocrisy, greed, self-serving interest and exploitation of people in the Lord's house, will bring God's judgment.

From the world's perspective, Jesus' actions hardly appear humble because they are not viewed through the lens of biblical humility. Jesus' humility is confirmed through his fierce loyalty to the person and will of his Father, coupled with radical obedience to uphold the Father's justice and holiness.

Jesus was *divisive*. He was fully aware that his teachings would divide those that believed, from those who wanted to remain in the rituals of man-focused religion.

> *"I am come to send fire on the earth; and what will I, if it be already kindled? But I have a baptism to be baptized with; and how am I straightened till it be accomplished! Suppose ye that I am come to give peace on earth? I tell you, Nay; but rather division: For from henceforth there shall be five in one house divided, three against two, and two against three. The father*

shall be divided against the son, and the son against the father; the mother against the daughter, and the daughter against the mother; the mother in law against her daughter in law, and the daughter in law against her mother in law" (Luke 12:49-53 KJV).

Unlike many in the body of Christ today, who try to appease people and make it easy for them to believe, Jesus demanded people's loyalty to the Truth above all else, including family allegiance. He didn't pursue compromise for the sake of preserving man-focused unity.

The Son of Man was *loving, merciful, and compassionate.* The most touching example of Jesus' merciful and compassionate love is illustrated in the woman caught in adultery in John Chapter 8. His compassionate manner contrasted the harsh approach of the Scribes and Pharisees. These rigid, religious leaders roughly handle this woman, bringing her publicly into the temple area and thrusting her into the midst of Jesus' teaching. They are concerned only with fulfilling the letter of the law against the woman, while the man in this circumstance, is not condemned. They also have a hidden agenda to trap Jesus into taking an unlawful stance, for they have seen his consummate compassion for the people.

Jesus perceives both their agenda and their self-righteous, rather than righteous judgment, which preserves the respect and the value of the individual. Jesus exudes softness in his unassuming, compassionate manner, in contrast to the brash and harsh Scribes and Pharisees. He defuses their hypocrisy with a simple statement. *"He that is without sin among you, let him first cast a stone at her" (John 8:7 KJV).*

After all slink away convicted by Jesus' statement, he turns to the woman and addresses her with tender dignity and gentle admonishment. *"Woman, where are those thine accusers? Hath no man condemned thee? She said, No man, Lord. And Jesus said unto her, neither do I condemn thee; go, and sin no more" (John 8:10-11 KJV).*

True humility preserves the dignity of the individual. It addresses issues and problems with love that is compassionate and merciful, while upholding both accountability and truth. True humility exposes hidden agendas and self-righteous, hypocritical behavior.

Jesus could be *patient, outwardly impatient and pointedly direct.* When the disciples were unable to cast out the demon spirit in a young boy, Jesus was clearly irritated. *Jesus said to them, "You faithless people! How long must I be with you? How long must I put up with you? Bring the boy to me'"* (Mark 6:19 NLT). He then patiently inquired about the problem. However, when the father of the boy in unbelief questioned his ability to cast the demon out, his response was tinged with frustration. *"What do you mean, if I can?" Jesus asked. "Anything is possible if a person believes"* (Mark 9:23 NLT).

Jesus demonstrated many facets of his humanness; yet, he was submitted to, and under the control of, a spirit of humility. He never allowed his humanness to interfere with his purpose—the supernatural work he was called to fulfill. He marveled at the faith of the centurion (Matthew 8:10), and was utterly disappointed at the numerous instances of lack of faith in his own disciples. He grieved that neither members of his own family, nor his hometown, believed in him. Stunned and disheartened by their rejection, his ministry marginalized, he lamented: …*"A prophet is honored everywhere except in his own hometown and among his own family." And so he did only a few miracles there because of their unbelief* (Matthew 13:57-58 NLT). However, none of these emotions distracted him. Neither did he fear their opinions, nor their estimation of him and his ministry.

Believers who are wearing their robe of righteousness are controlled by a spirit of humility. They will baffle the world, but bring glory to the God they serve wholeheartedly. In the end, humility is what *separates* true servants of God from those who are self-serving, trapped in religious pretense and the fear of man.

Chapter 3

CALLED TO UNITY

Without unity, a supernatural work will not manifest. Scripturally the mandate is clear *"...and every city or house divided against itself shall not stand"* (Matthew 12:25 KJV). From the world's perspective, vision is primary; but in God's kingdom unity is foremost. Unity in the kingdom is different than unity in the world.

Culturally, we equate unity with the absence of strife—meaning we are getting along at a superficial level. Moreover, those under our authority are acquiescing to our will and rule. This type of unity is merely the suppression of our personal will, to achieve the specific objective of the group. It does not mean we are philosophically in alignment with the goal; however, it does mean we agree to do our part to achieve the end result.

On the contrary, when we function in the unity of the Spirit, we are operating from our spirit not our flesh. The flesh cannot create unity of the Spirit; it is divinely imparted (Romans 8:8). The Spirit of Unity is imparted as we surrender our will to the work of the Holy Spirit, and submit our minds to the truth. To achieve unity of Spirit, requires loyalty to the truth and remaining in step with the Holy Spirit.

Unity of the Spirit allows for questioning, disagreement, and for challenging the status quo. Rather than harm the bonds of unity, these strengthen the union because they are integral to fellowship and freedom. True unity only exists in an environment that does not punish the intellect, the inquisitiveness, the creativity and the discernment of the body. The reason is that the individuals function as an interdependently connected group, not as independent or co-dependent individuals. As we are properly related to others, we experience freedom and find fulfillment. However, as independent or co-dependent, we are in a debilitating bondage that does not provide for free choice. We either mindlessly follow another, or become a slave to our own independence. In interdependency, we are in unity with others, in a mutual exchange relationship in which we receive and give.

The oneness of the Spirit flows through the bond of peace. Paul exhorted the Ephesians: *"I, therefore, the prisoner of the Lord, beseech you, that ye walk worthy of the vocation wherewith ye are called. With all lowliness and meekness, and with longsuffering, forbearing one another in love. Endeavoring to keep the unity of the Spirit in the bond of peace"* (Ephesians 4:1-3 KJV). While unity of the Spirit is imparted, it is maintained through love that is bathed in grace and humility. This love, clothed in grace and humility, is possible when we dwell in his presence and are interdependently connected.

In divine unity exists a unity of authority, order and structure. The bond of peace is freedom from striving and controlling. Through fellowship in the Holy Spirit the work is accomplished.

Drivers on an interstate reflect the concept of unity. For the traffic to flow efficiently and effectively cars must remain in their lanes. Everyone is headed in the same direction but not necessarily at the same speed or timing; nor do they all have the same assignment. The highway patrol is the authority; order is maintained through speed limits and road signs; all motorists operate within the structure of the highway system of lanes, exits and entrance ramps. If all motorists stay in the lanes and follow the order of speed limits and road signage, there is freedom for all to travel to their destinations without striving or controlling other drivers.

THREE CATEGORIES OF BELIEVERS

We, as believers, are on the highway of holiness—to be established in unity is to drive in the freedom of Christ interdependently connected to those on the road with us. However, some believers are tailgaters following someone else on the highway too closely. Or conversely, others drive independently, switching lanes at will, and disregarding the signage, speed limits and the right-of-way of other motorists on the road.

Co-dependent

Individuals who are co-dependent function as though they have no capacity of their own. They communicate in a manner that speaks to others *"I have nothing of value to give."* Consequently, they look to others as their source. Intellectually they understand they are unique and no one can contribute what they alone have to offer—unfortunately, they do not *believe* it in their spirit. **They tend to be unbalanced to one extreme or the other on a *contributor/receiver* continuum.**

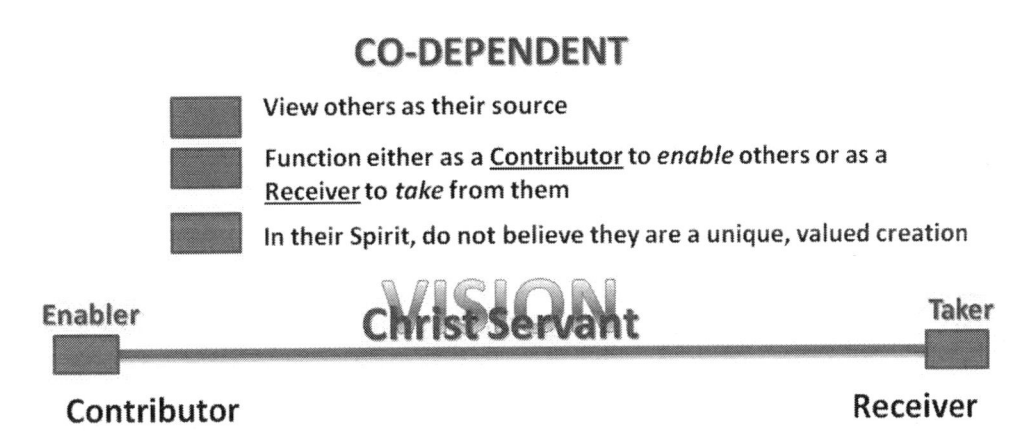

CO-DEPENDENT

- View others as their source
- Function either as a <u>Contributor</u> to *enable* others or as a <u>Receiver</u> to *take* from them
- In their Spirit, do not believe they are a unique, valued creation

Enabler	Christ Servant	Taker
Contributor		**Receiver**

Individuals in the *contributor* mode mostly operate in "helping" with this or that. They do not perceive themselves as worthy unless they are *enabling* others. This precipitates an unhealthy pattern where they do not assist in order for others to achieve rather they over-compensate in the helping area to the detriment of a healthy give-and-take relationship. The opposite end of the spectrum is the *receiver* who continually expects others to take responsibility for his/her nurture and growth.

Religious teaching on spiritual gifts somewhat fosters co-dependency. Instead of encouraging believers to function in many gifts, the instruction is to focus on one area of gifting and then to view oneself in terms of that one gifting. For example, if an individual possesses the gift of "helps" they are relegated to the area of hospitality. This same individual may also have a prophetic gifting but it will remain underdeveloped because the person is only viewed, supported and directed toward serving others because this gift is prominent. In the case of a co-dependent individual at the *contributor* end of the spectrum, his or her tendency will be to enable others while God may be calling him/her to exercise a dormant prophetic gift. This approach may actually bring believers into bondage, and in many instances, can be a form of control.

Independent

Independent individuals view contribution, participation and aspects of their role in terms of personal impact. They tend to operate from a position of how circumstances and people personally affect them. This mode of operation is based on a *self-serving* model not the servant model of the kingdom.

Independent individuals are not rightly related to the corporate body nor can they embody the vision. For example, when we think and reason based on our old nature (putting the self first), we remain in bondage. Our old way of thinking constrains us and we do not receive all that we are destined to become in Christ. We will be sidetracked by circumstances and people that inhibit our desires or needs. As Christ servants we are carriers of the vision. We are not striving to achieve an "entity" outside of ourselves. If we are filled with *self* there is no room within our spirit for the vision to reside. We experience the yo-yo effect of seating self on the throne of our heart whenever someone or something threatens our equilibrium.

Another perspective of self-serving is getting caught up in the teachings and experiences of Christ in which we seek experiential knowledge and revelation knowledge but we keep it to ourselves, neglecting to fellowship and share our experiences and knowledge with others. We are taking everything in but not giving out to others—we lack concern about other believers' spiritual walk; we merely maintain our own.

If we operate from a renewed mind, we have the freedom to be creative, to make choices, to experience the fullness of God—this brings us into the unity of the Spirit. We prayerfully stay in our lane; we focus on our appointment and fulfill our assignment in the bond of unity. People who are independent or co-dependent focus on the "vessel" either themselves or another person not the vessel-maker.

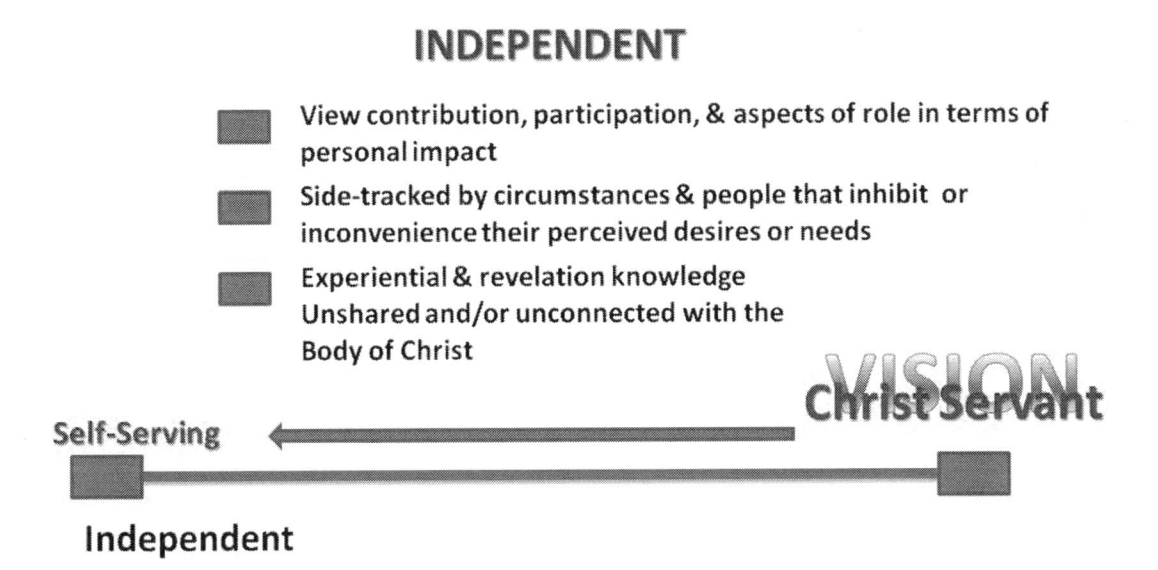

INDEPENDENT

- View contribution, participation, & aspects of role in terms of personal impact
- Side-tracked by circumstances & people that inhibit or inconvenience their perceived desires or needs
- Experiential & revelation knowledge Unshared and/or unconnected with the Body of Christ

Self-Serving ←———————————— Christ Servant VISION

Independent

REBELLIOUS SPIRIT

A pitfall of an independent spirit is that without full submission to the Holy Spirit, the individual will operate under the demonic influence of a control spirit or rebellious spirit, which the scriptures identify as witchcraft. Israel's King Saul is a biblical example of an individual with an independent spirit who functioned under the control of a rebellious spirit.

In 1 Samuel chapter 15, King Saul who had been instructed by the Lord to completely destroy the Amalekite nation, instead chose to allow the best of the livestock, booty, and the Amalekite king to be spared. Saul then made excuses for his disobedience and blamed the people saying that his troops demanded he spare the livestock and the loot to sacrifice to the Lord. An independent spirit will always seek to deflect responsibility and make excuses for his or her actions and behavior. However, the prophet Samuel confronted Saul with the truth despite his affection and friendship with the king.

So Samuel said: "Has the LORD as great delight in burnt offerings and sacrifices, As in obeying the voice of the LORD? Behold, to obey is better than sacrifice, And to heed than the fat of rams.

For rebellion is as the sin of witchcraft, And stubbornness is as iniquity and idolatry. Because you have rejected the word of the LORD, He also has rejected you from being king." (1 Samuel 15:22-23 NKJV).

<u>*Dealing with a control/rebellious spirit*</u>. If not addressed, an independent spirit will derail a supernatural work as it provides an entrance for demonic control. It produces a legal entry to infuse the work with elements of darkness—jealousy, envy, and dissension, as James clearly articulates, *For where envying and strife is, there is confusion and every evil work (James 3:16 KJV).* Therefore, a rebellious spirit must be dealt with immediately by applying the appropriate consequences. As noted above, Samuel addressed Saul's excuses for what they were—disobedience. He then informed Saul of the consequences, the Lord had rejected him as king.

In short, the Lord will not rule where idols dwell. A rebellious person's allegiance is to a spirit of witchcraft—an idol. Further, they operate from a self-serving model, thus idolizing themselves! The root spirit is a *spirit of rejection*. The spirit of rejection provides a breeding ground for insecurity, offense, and an insatiable need for acceptance and approval. The independent spirit can manifest as aggression. The individual will continually strive with others fostering an environment of competition, one up-man-ship, and rivalry. Similarly, a rebellious spirit can manifest as self-absorption. Self-absorbed individuals remain separate and focused on their own needs and interests unable to function interdependently with the group. They seek to do their "own thing" which has been sanctioned by God (according to them) and therefore, they need not come under any delegated authority.

A leader of a supernatural work addresses a rebellious spirit by placing the individual in a safe and supportive environment to confront the situation. The objective is to pose questions that uncover to the individual the exact nature and root of the problem. Our goal in a supernatural work is to honor and respect the individual while *allowing the Holy Spirit to lift the veil of deception or to confront knowing disobedience*. In this environment, the individual has the freedom to choose to be interdependently connected. Many believers, when they discover the root of their rebellion, rather than being confronted with the result of their rebellious actions, seek repentance and restoration.

If the person submits to the work of the Holy Spirit and repents of coming under a spirit of witchcraft, he or she needs to be aware that this spirit has not only affected them personally, but all those to whom they are connected. Witchcraft is a root spirit so other spirits are attached to it; therefore, we command all associated spirits to bow and come out of the person as the dominant spirit is uprooted.

As relationships are identified, the person begins to understand the permeating effects of sin and his or her responsibility to preserve and restore those relationships. As the leader and co-leaders help the person work through this process, a plan of restoration will emerge. It will require humility and obedience on the part of the individual to deal with the consequences of their rebellious behavior. The person must seek out the impacted groups and individuals for forgiveness and restoration, addressing issues and wrongs.

On the contrary, should the person deny the problem or counterattack, remove the person from the work. Removing the person from the work must be done with all gentleness and humility giving every opportunity for the Holy Spirit to enlighten the individual of the darkness to which he or she has become bound.

Relinquishing a rebellious—independent spirit. In prayer, bring the person to the feet of Jesus. Sitting in this position of humility, ask the person to *yield* his/her will to the will of the Father. Yielding the will changes the individual's focus from self to God. In this place of submission, the soul is transformed—it is changed from an earthly to a heavenly focus. While these steps are sequential, they are not final in terms of a one-time surrender. The individual will need to persevere and remain proactive to restore relationships, renew his or her mindset and change independent behaviors and actions.

1. Reject the Spirit of Witchcraft—with the co-habiting spirits of rebellion and rejection. The curse of witchcraft is broken and cast out of his/her temple. The individual is no longer under the influence of demonic spirits and now this dark place is to be filled with the Holy Spirit.

2. The second step is to freely surrender his/her thoughts and desires to assume the Father's. In *yielding our will to the Father*, we are *restored* to His original intent for our life. This positions the person in the place of blessing where God's plan and purpose for their destiny can manifest.

3. The *root* problem has been identified through the questioning process. The root is what initiated the descent into rebellion. The person will be instrumental in defining the solution to the problems/issues that have resulted because of the root problem.

4. The individual must not just *admit* their issues and sins—but repent— overcome them! Repent means to change not to continue in the behavior and be sorry for it. Stop blaming others and making excuses. Take responsibility for their behavior and actions.

5. Rely on God, trust him and his Word. Ask the person to relinquish his/her own opinion, and the fear of man, and take on the *Mind of Christ*. This means he or she is abandoning all self-reliance and self-centeredness.

6. Next, the person is to <u>stop</u> *praying* about the situation/person/problem and start DOING! It is time to begin the process of forgiveness and restoration. Praying over and over about the same problem is a way independent spirits deflect responsibility. This type of prayer is but a passive means of not taking responsibility or accountability to resolve relational, project, or personal issues.

7. As a group, guide and support the individual in developing a reconciliation and restoration plan. Throughout this process, we honor the individual as a child of the King, who is willing to come into alignment with the Truth and truly be set free. Our objective is to bring forth the destiny for which this person was created.

The process outlined above is the beginning of walking in the Spirit. Over time, fruit will be evident in their lives of the internal change. If they have truly repented and submitted to His will and delegated authority, they will proactively seek to restore their connections to others and begin functioning interdependently.

Interdependent

Interdependent individuals operate through mutual exchange—in two-way relationships. They view themselves as part of a whole and desire to contribute their portion while supporting the contributions of others. This frees every individual to fulfill their assignment in the supernatural work.

Interdependence promotes trust as it allows for dissension without destroying the bond of unity. An interdependent individual's source of sustaining power is Christ. Allowing Christ to work through us, we work together embodying the vision and the divine purpose. Trust breeds peace and not confusion. Peace initiates unity and counteracts negativity. Thus, people stay in their lane when it is difficult, when they disagree, when they're weary and when the road takes an unexpected or sharp turn into unfamiliar territory. They stay the course—persevere—press on toward the goal—because it (the supernatural work) is not about them; rather it is his purpose and his glory they are pursuing.

How do we function interdependently? It is not always about us or not about another person—it is foremost about Christ. He must be our focus so that we stay in unity and perform our assignment for his glory.

INTERDEPENDENT

- Operate through mutual exchange, in two-way relationships
- Christ is their source and sustaining power
- Function in the Unity of the Spirit that creates the environment for people to stay in their lane

Support & Encourage	VISION / Christ Servant	Mutual Give & Take
Contributor	⟷	Receiver

VISION

Contrary to the ways of the world, a supernatural work builds unity of the Spirit first. When we are in alignment with the Spirit, the heavens will be opened to us and we will walk in the fullness of our anointing. To move in vision before the anointing and the opening of the heavens will cause striving in the flesh creating an opening for Satan to enter the work. This is scriptural. For 30 years Jesus walked the earth prior to his baptism, however, he did not walk in the fullness of his anointing, including walking in signs and wonders, until the heavens were opened and the Spirit descended in fullness upon him.

> *When He had been baptized, Jesus came up immediately from the water; and behold, the heavens were opened to Him, and He saw the Spirit of God descending like a dove and alighting upon Him. And suddenly a voice came from heaven, saying, "This is My beloved Son, in whom I am well pleased." (Matthew 3:16-17 NKJV).*

Jesus, in unity with and in fullness of the Spirit, began his ministry. He then selected his disciples revealing that he was the promised Messiah. Nonetheless, he did not speak the vision (his death and subsequent resurrection) to his disciples immediately. Rather, he fellowshipped with them, teaching them about the kingdom and bringing them into unity with the Godhead. For most of their ministry with Jesus, the disciples did not understand his message, nor why he was doing the things he did. Therefore, they had no clear vision for much of the three years they ministered alongside of Jesus.

This lack of clarity around the vision is difficult for us to understand. We have adopted the world's paradigm of vision. From the world's perspective, a *vision is an aspirational description of what the organization desires to achieve or accomplish in the long term*. It represents a desired future that is outside of us. We focus our energies and resources to pursue it.

Contrarily, in the kingdom, the vision is *inside* of us; it can only be achieved as we come into unity of the Spirit. We are carriers of the vision. Kingdom visions are spiritual and not external. The vision does not take us to a destination, but a person—Christ. It is not a conforming process, but a transforming process—we are to be transformed into his image. *But we all, with unveiled face, beholding as in a mirror the glory of the Lord, are being transformed into the same image from glory to glory, just as by the Spirit of the Lord* (2 Corinthians 3:18 NKJV).

The most common failure of works in the body of Christ is people run with a vision but have not come into unity of the Spirit. They are pursuing a destination, not a person. Consequently, they seek to achieve an objective outside of themselves, rather than internalizing the vision, and waiting for it as Habakkuk describes: *For the vision is yet for an appointed time; But at the end it will speak, and it will not lie. Though it tarries, wait for it; Because it will surely come, It will not tarry* (Habakkuk 2:3 NKJV).

The vision cannot speak to us until its appointed time—until we are one with the Spirit. We cannot move out in vision before the appointed time. We must tarry—come into the unity of the Spirit, so that the vision can manifest within us, the power and anointing to fulfill the work.

These things I have spoken to you in figurative language; but the time is coming when I will no longer speak to you in figurative language, but I will tell you plainly about the Father. In that day you will ask in My name, and I do not say to you that I shall pray the Father for you; for the Father Himself loves you, because you have loved Me, and have believed that I came forth from God. I came forth from the Father and have come into the world. Again, I leave the world and go to the Father."

His disciples said to Him, "See, now You are speaking plainly, and using no figure of speech! Now we are sure that You know all things, and have no need that anyone should question You. By this we believe that You came forth from God."

Jesus answered them, "Do you now believe? Indeed the hour is coming, yes, has now come, that you will be scattered, each to his own, and will leave Me alone. And yet I am not alone, because the Father is with Me. These things I have spoken to you, that in Me you may have peace. In the world you will have tribulation; but be of good cheer, I have overcome the world" (John 16:25-33 NKJV).

In the above passage, at the very end of Jesus' earthly ministry, the disciples had finally come to the place of unity of the Spirit where Christ could begin to truly reveal the vision to them. However, as yet, they did not have the fullness of the Spirit—the anointing. Jesus instructed them in Luke 24:49 (NKJV): *"Behold, I send the Promise of My Father upon you; but tarry in the city of Jerusalem until you are endued with power from on high."* The disciples (governing leaders) were commanded to wait on the vision until they had received the fullness of the Spirit—the anointing of power before moving out in the vision.

In Acts 2 (NKJV), after having tarried in unity of the Spirit for 40 days, the Spirit descended upon them in fullness—with the power and anointing of Jesus; the heavens opened and they began walking in signs and wonders as carriers of the vision.

When the Day of Pentecost had fully come, they were all with one accord in one place. And suddenly there came a sound from heaven, as of a rushing mighty wind, and it filled the whole house where they were sitting. Then there appeared to them divided tongues, as of fire, and one sat upon each of them. And they were all filled with the Holy Spirit and began to speak with other tongues, as the Spirit gave them utterance (vs. 1-4).

And with many other words he testified and exhorted them, saying, "Be saved from this perverse generation." Then those who gladly received his word were baptized; and that day about three thousand souls were added to them. And they continued steadfastly in the apostles' doctrine and fellowship, in the breaking of bread, and in prayers. Then fear came upon every soul, and many wonders and signs were done through the apostles (vs. 40-43).

Henceforth, the disciples were carriers of the vision—they had internalized it, becoming ever more transformed into his image. They now carried the fulfillment of the vision within them. They had become the church of which Jesus prophesied: *"And I also say to you that you are Peter, and on this rock I will build My church, and the gates of Hades shall not prevail against it"* (Matthew 16:18 NKJV). They had moved from the natural to the supernatural. They were purged of all earthy ambition and reliance on their own abilities. That is the purpose of a kingdom vision—to bring us to the place where Satan has nothing in us. We are seated in heavenly places with Christ Jesus. We follow his protocol and build according to the blueprints of heaven because they have become our DNA.

The graphic below depicts the vision as *internal,* not a destination. We are not moving the co-laborers toward the vision; we are moving them toward the Godhead. The process will transform us into the image of Christ. As we internalize the vision, the mission is those things we see the Father doing.

If Jesus is our model, he operated fluidly in his mission. For instance, a Canaanite woman pleaded with Jesus to heal her demon-possessed daughter (Matthew 15:21-28). Although, he said his mission was only to the House of Israel, she continued to plead with him to heal her daughter. Jesus, recognized what the Father was doing—responding to the woman's faith. Jesus spoke the word and her daughter was healed that very hour. This demonstrates how kingdom vision and mission are transforming not conforming.

KINGDOM MODEL—VISION & MISSION LEAD TO THE GODHEAD

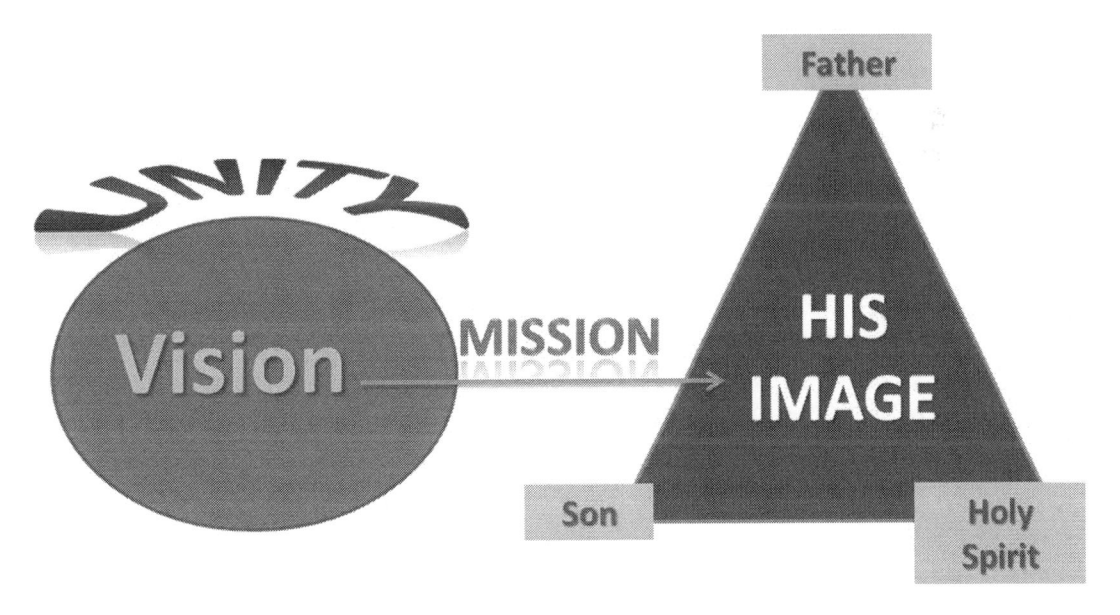

In summary, in God's kingdom, we seek unity of the Spirit above all else. This is our primary focus. If we move into our mission without the unity of the Spirit, we are unable to internalize the vision. Our focus will be distorted, for the vision does not speak until its appointed time — when we have come into unity with the Spirit. This unity brings us into alignment with heaven, so that the power and anointing of the supernatural manifests. Otherwise, as leaders, we will move the organization toward "something," as opposed to, toward "someone" — the Godhead. We will build, yet another structure of the world, rather than birthing into the world that which was designed and blueprinted in the heavenly realm.

As we build, we recognize we are interconnected; we foster an environment that honors interdependence and the diverse anointings in the organization; however, we do not support the "lone ranger" approach of independents, or protect and enable co-dependents by coddling them. Our goal is to grow the people into his image. The avenue for this growth is to function interdependently — in two-way relationships in which Christ is both our source and sustaining power. We are not dependent upon people; rather, we are interdependently connected with them. In other words, I cannot fulfill my assignment without you, and you cannot fulfill your part without me. When this becomes the "mindset," people stay the course and unify to achieve a purpose beyond themselves. They stay in their lane, because that is where God has positioned them, not man. They persevere because they are building God's kingdom for his glory not a reputation or fiefdom of their own.

Chapter 4

THE ANOINTING

In the last chapter we discovered that unity of the Spirit is pivotal to a supernatural work. Without unity, we lack the manifestation of the Spirit or the anointing. *The anointing is the power and presence of God manifested in a committed vessel yielded to the Holy Spirit.*

The Scripture decrees that the anointing breaks the yoke (Isaiah 10:27). A yoke is anything that constrains us; keeps us in a place of bondage. These are mindsets and structures of the world. God is creative. To operate in the anointing, we must break out of the mindsets and structures of the world. To be anointed is to get out of the box of religion and into a relationship with the living God.

BECOMING AN ANOINTED VESSEL

An anointed vessel is a dwelling place of God. His temple is established within us—we become his habitation. In this place of dwelling, we tabernacle with him.

To understand what it means to tabernacle with God, we must look at the tabernacle of Moses. In Exodus 25:8 & 22 KJV, God instructs Moses: *"And let them make me a **sanctuary**; that I may dwell among them. (v.22) And there I will meet with thee, and I will **commune** with thee from above the mercy seat, and from between the two cherubims which are upon the ark of the testimony, of all things which I will give thee in commandment unto the children of Israel"* (emphasis added). Moses and the Israelites constructed this edifice exactly as God instructed. It consisted of an outer court, an inner court and the holy of holies. The Hebrew word *miqdash*[1] is translated as sanctuary. It means a consecrated place, especially a palace or asylum, chapel or holy place. To commune, *dabar*[2] in the Hebrew means to speak, declare, promise, pronounce, be a spokesman, talk, teach, think, use entreaties and utter.

As God promised, he met with Moses in the tabernacle:

And it came to pass, when Moses went out unto the tabernacle, that all the people rose up, and stood every man at his tent door, and looked after Moses, until he was gone into the tabernacle. And it came to pass, as Moses entered into the tabernacle, the cloudy pillar descended, and stood at the door of the tabernacle, and the Lord talked with Moses. And all the people saw the cloudy pillar stand at the tabernacle door: and all the people rose up and worshipped, every man in his tent door. And the LORD spake unto Moses face to face, as a man speaketh unto his friend. And he turned again into the camp: but his servant Joshua, the son of Nun, a young man, departed not out of the tabernacle (Exodus 33:8-11 KJV).

When we tabernacle with God, we *move* into deeper, more intimate relationship with him. We begin in the *outer court* where the Spirit begins to dismantle strongholds constructed in our minds through our natural reasoning. We progress through the *inner court* where God deals with our idols. We must sacrifice our idols on the altar—everything that hinders us from becoming wholly his (career, family, money, selfish desires, material things, etc.). In the inner court, we are purified through fire. The Lord removes all the dross from our lives. *And I will turn my hand upon thee, and purely purge away thy dross, and take away all thy tin* (Isaiah 1:25 KJV). For a season, at different intervals in our walk with the Lord, we return to this place as he reveals dark places in our soul—rejection, unforgiveness, woundedness that must be exposed to the Light and healed.

Finally, the way is opened to enter the *holy of holies* where the Ark of the Covenant, or the very presence of God, inhabits our being. In this place, God imparts the anointing. His Spirit communes with our spirit—imparting his thoughts and purposes. He anoints us to be his spokesman to declare, decree, teach, and pronounce his purpose, promises and prophetic utterances.

Moses fellowshipped with God in the tabernacle, and the glory cloud descended; the glory cloud is the manifestation of God's presence. In his presence, he reveals the pattern, the strategy and the protocol of your assignment. In the glory cloud, everything happens instantaneously—healing, deliverance, miracles. There is no striving as all the attributes of the Holy Spirit are flowing—*the Spirit upon, wisdom and understanding, counsel and might, knowledge and fear of the Lord* (Isaiah 11:2).

The anointing empowers us to *move* in the full expression of the Holy Spirit. To complete a supernatural work, all the attributes are required and are supernaturally imparted in the anointing. The anointing resembles an explosion of the Spirit such that revelation knowledge flows, bondages are broken, healing and prophetic words of *what is to come* manifest. All things are possible because the "yoke" of unbelief (man's reasoning) is broken and our vessel is totally surrendered to be a conduit of God's power.

Operating in the anointing is like having a full orchestra within you. The Holy Spirit can impart whatever is needed in that moment, in that particular situation. With the fullness—the richness and unity of sound reverberate, breaking the yoke of Satan, unlike the hollow sound of our own abilities. We become just clanging cymbals—making noise in the natural, but the strongholds in the spiritual realm are not dismantled.

Many believers are waiting on a move of God, when we carry the move within us. Like Moses we are seeking the glory cloud for the pattern; in the anointing—the move is already there, we must flow in it.

Character

The anointing has both enthralled and perplexed the body of Christ. For the most part, it has been described in such nebulous terms that believers cannot truly fathom what constitutes the anointing. The anointing is the manifestation of the power (dunamis) of God. *Dunamis*[3] is a Greek word which means miraculous power and ability. *It is a power that transcends our natural abilities and supernaturally transforms physical, emotional, and intellectual states. It is the creative essence of God manifested through a human vessel.* The dunamis is the *resurrection power* that raised Christ from the dead (Rom. 1:4; Phil. 3:10). There is no comparable power in the earthly realm that brings to life that which was dead, and creates into being that which was not!

> *But you shall receive power ("dunamis") - ability, efficiency and might - when the Holy Spirit has come upon you; and you shall be My witnesses in Jerusalem and all Judea and Samaria and to the ends - the very bounds - of the earth"* (Acts 1:8 AMP, emphasis added).

When we receive the Holy Spirit, this power begins operating in us. However, the measure of the power that can be released through us is dependent upon the fullness of our surrender to the Spirit's work within us. *"Now all glory to God, who is able, through his mighty power at work within us, to accomplish infinitely more than we might ask or think* (Ephesians 3:20 NLT).

Our unbelief, or the absence of faith in others, will hinder the manifestation of the power of God through us. Jesus encountered this obstruction in Capernaum because of the people's unbelief. *Then Jesus told them, "A prophet is honored everywhere except in his own hometown and among his own family." And so he (Jesus) did only a few miracles there because of their unbelief* (Matthew 13:57-58 NLT, emphasis added).

In God's design, dunamis is to function in holiness; thus, we must possess a Godly character in proportion to the anointing we carry. Jesus is our example of dunamis released through Godly character. Jesus was *…declared to be the Son of God with power, according to the spirit of holiness, by the resurrection from the dead: By whom we have received grace and apostleship, for obedience to the faith among all nations, for his name* (Romans 1:4-5 KJV).

Virtually all of the spiritual train wrecks recorded of anointed vessels in the body of Christ, were the result of the vessels not possessing the level of character equal to the anointing they carried. This is not the fault of the Creator. As we have demonstrated in earlier chapters, God chooses us and then begins to mold and shape us into his image. However, it is our responsibility to cooperate with this process of cleansing, purging and breaking. This is God's *character building* process.

When the power of God is *functioning* in our lives, it will produce holiness, for we begin to see through God's eyes. His standard is what we uphold, not the cultural norms around us. Our character is molded by his image that we carry within us, and the "dunamis" gives us the ability to deal with undisciplined behavior, unbelief, and insensitive heart attitudes.

The Dunamis Power and Word Connection of the Anointing

As God dwells within us—the Word is resident in our Spirit. As we read and meditate on God's Word, the Holy Spirit illumines the Word in prayer, in sharing or reading of it and we receive a rhema revelation. How much *dunamis*—resurrection power is released is proportional to how much of the Word we have received into our Spirit, *not just read*, and are walking in it. The more indwelling of the Word in you, the greater is the level of resurrection power released through you. Think of it in terms of the space Christ (the Word) occupies in your heart; that is exactly how much of the resurrection power is working through you. A yielded, submitted vessel carries tremendous power.

As God's Word does not return void—so the strength of the power of what you speak is also exponentially increased. We must be very careful of what we speak. It will come to fruition whether for good or evil. What we have failed to realize is that we are determining it—not the enemy or God. We are making the choice to speak in alignment with the enemy or God.

Many anointed vessels, at the height of their destiny, became too casual with the dunamis they carried. As a result, they suffered the consequences of careless words spoken in presumption or taunting. We do not mock the enemy. I (Jan) have heard from the pulpit, on more than one occasion, an anointed vessel voice a taunt such as "Come after me devil, just try it!" It may have been spoken in jest or to stir a reaction from the audience, but those words are backed with *resurrection power*—the person was speaking under the anointing! To illustrate, Job sadly realized, *"For the thing I greatly feared has come upon me, And what I dreaded has happened to me"* (Job 3:25 NKJV). Job unwittingly spoke and prayed his fears not faith. . . .*For Job said, "It may be that my sons have sinned and cursed God in their hearts." Thus Job did regularly* (Job 1:5 KJV). Fear is a spirit. When Job spoke from fear, not faith, he created an entrance point for the enemy; he knew exactly where and how to attack Job.

The anointing is precious and not to be treated lightly. Rather we carry it in reverential fear of the Lord as a treasure.

THE ANOINTED STRUCTURE

When yokes are broken God elevates. *"For it shall come to pass in that day, saith the LORD of hosts, that I will break his yoke from off thy neck, and will burst thy bonds, and strangers shall no more serve themselves of him: But they shall serve the LORD their God, and David their king, whom I will raise up unto them"* (Jeremiah 30:8-9 KJV).

In birthing a new work, God chooses his instrument(s). Just as every child created in the womb is unique, so is every instrument used by God in a supernatural work. They are distinctive in that they do not conform to the status quo—they reach for the high calling in Christ Jesus. They are purged vessels—willing to break with tradition to obey the Spirit. Above all else, they seek intimacy with God. These vessels have died to carnal ambition and the love of material things. They are committed to the Lord regardless of the cost, and do not measure success by results.

In God's structure, we operate in a kingdom where he is King. Kingdoms are not democracies. When we received Christ as our personal savior we were transferred from the Kingdom of Darkness (where Satan rules) into the Kingdom of Light (where Christ rules). If we operate through the world's paradigm—we are little kings in our own kingdom. At least that's what we think, although we are merely puppets, with Satan pulling the strings as we sacrifice our all on the altar of ambition, pleasure, materialism, children, religion—whatever our idol may be. What has become normal in the body of Christ is to speak in terms of democracy, where majority rules and we have a voice in the system. Truth is, in a democracy, we are still controlled and manipulated by dominant groups that have access and control over the required resources.

As we operate in God's kingdom, we must change our democratic mindsets. God is in control of everything—people and resources! God is supreme ruler and all other leadership is *appointed* not voted in by popularity or ability. This perspective is shocking and revolting to much of the body of Christ! Mentally, we assent to our kingdom status; however, we live as believers as though we are ruled by a democracy. Thus, we vacillate between two extremes—jockeying for position, or through false humility, believing that none should be exalted. Neither perspective is biblical.

In God's kingdom, he chooses the leader of his divine work. This is his pattern throughout the Bible, from Abraham in the Old Testament, to the Apostle Paul in the New Testament. In I Samuel 16:6-7(KJV), God gives us his criteria for choosing David as king over Israel: *And it came to pass, when they were come, that he looked on Eliab, and said, Surely the LORD's anointed is before him. But the LORD said unto Samuel, Look not on his countenance, or on the height of his stature; because I have refused him: for the LORD seeth not as man seeth; for man looketh on the outward appearance, but the LORD looketh on the heart.* God's choice is based on the heart—and only God knows our heart.

Once God *calls* a leader—He will "break" him or her. He alone knows what will derail, distract and destroy us. Only those willing to go through the breaking process are *chosen*. If we stop short, we will disqualify ourselves—as Satan will have an opening to come in to rob, kill and destroy. Or, what we started in the Spirit, we will be tempted to complete in our flesh—neither alternative is acceptable to God, and the assignment will be transferred to another *submitted* vessel. Or, if we repent, as in the case of David's adultery with Bathsheba, we can retain our appointment but will suffer the consequences of our disobedience.

Additionally, in a kingdom structure *all* leadership is appointed. In a later chapter, we will discuss leadership appointments. Again, we must dismantle our worldly mindsets if we are to co-labor in birthing a supernatural work, and begin to operate in structure and leadership from a kingdom perspective.

Charismatic Witchcraft

Man's structure promotes domination by demonic spirits. Man's structure will feed into a hierarchy that emphasizes position and span of control. Those within these structures can easily fall prey to operating outside of the Holy Spirit anointing. They begin to operate in a counterfeit spirit called charismatic witchcraft. *Charismatic witchcraft* is rooted in human charisma. It is a counterfeit authority that operates through manipulation, control and man-pleasing influences that displace the Holy Spirit. The parallel can be so subtle that without the fullness of the Spirit operating in our vessels, we are unable to discern the difference. Whole movements and works within the church have been taken over by this counterfeit spirit.

This counterfeit spirit can be discerned whenever motives are driven by domination, manipulation, intimidation and emotional blackmail. These areas were identified in an internet article titled *Charismatic Witchcraft*[2] and are expanded below.

Domination. Domination is not to be confused with a strong personality. This spirit can be discerned where the *motive* behind the actions of an individual or a group is to *conquer*. The motivation is conquest for the sake of ruling over an individual or group. The fruit produced is control over behavior, thinking and resources that stifles creativity, ownership and dissent in any form. Access to relationship and resources is predicated on submission to the dominant group. Any departure from the group norms is viewed as betrayal or disloyalty. It is punished by exclusion from meaningful participation and decision-making and/or isolation — distancing of other members from the offending group member.

Manipulation. Manipulation is the self-promoting use of position, power or influence to dictate an outcome in order to enhance one's fame, reputation or kingdom. Those operating in this spirit displace the Holy Spirit as the convictor and judge. Operating in a spirit of manipulation blinds an individual to alternative points of view, interpretations and ways of doing. The motive of manipulation is always *control* — of people, information, resources, and/or situations. Manipulation is the spirit behind knowing the truth, yet misapplying it to maintain one's point-of-view, status or position in the eyes of man.

Intimidation. Intimidation is a spirit. If we do not stand in our authority Satan will usurp it! He can only take our authority if we let him. One way he accomplishes this is to get our focus on man. Either through *fear of man* — what will they think? How will I be perceived? etc., or through *man-pleasing* — "I don't feel this is right, but if I want to stay on good terms with this group, I must do what I'm asked and acquiesce to their desires." This is intimidation! It causes the person being intimidated to feel insignificant, or *less than* in the sight of others. He or she must join in, or be viewed as ignorant or "siding" with the other side.

There is a difference between a persuasive and passionate appeal and using intimidation. The apostle Paul was persuasive. People were offended at the truth Paul preached, but he did not intimidate the unbelieving. Paul allowed the Holy Spirit to reveal truth; he did not intimidate his audience into believing. We cross the line and usurp the Holy Spirit's authority, when our words or actions coerce others to go along with our ideas or decisions.

Many in leadership use their authority to pressure followers to accept what they say or do, or condone what is said or done. Intimidation is intended to keep others in line and obedient, rather than in unity.

Emotional Blackmail. This spirit makes an appeal to an emotion with the intent that the person using the emotion is accurate or right merely because they make the accusation. This spirit often operates in situations and relationships where the individual emotionally blackmailing fears losing something they value highly — reputation, love, power, position, etc. Emotional appeals are generally put forward without context or genuine knowledge. Emotion is used to manipulate, intimidate and dominate to obtain one's desire. Emotional appeals and answers tend to focus on *selected facts,* not the whole truth; and therefore, appear to be evasive, and can lead to unjust conclusions.

We must search our own heart to discern whether we are displacing the Holy Spirit and operating out of charismatic witchcraft. Much can be accomplished through the flesh of human charisma, but it will neither last nor have the stamp of approval of God. Therefore, in eternity it will be burned up lacking any reward. A supernatural work of God is a high calling that is fulfilled through the anointing of the Holy Spirit for his glory.

In the past, we may have allowed ourselves to perpetrate or have been subject to these areas of Charismatic witchcraft, repent of your own involvement or participation. Then ask God to "seal" you and fortify your standing in him. *Grieve not the Holy Spirit of God whereby ye are sealed until the day of redemption* (Eph. 4:30 KJV). Charismatic witchcraft grieves and displaces the Holy Spirit; however, our repentance brings us back into fellowship and alignment with the Holy Spirit and God's divine purpose.

THE POWER TOOL

We have discovered in this chapter that the anointing is the "power tool" in building a supernatural work. If we do not constrain the spirit by operating in the mindset and structures of the world, God's spirit will move creatively through us to accomplish more than we could ask or think (Ephesians 3:20-21). Our part is to continually deepen our relationship with the Lord and grow evermore Christ-like in character, so that we walk worthy of the anointing we carry. The anointing is precious and flows through a kingdom structure. We prostitute the anointing into charismatic witchcraft when we attempt to flow in it through worldly structures that emphasize position and control. Without a conscious awareness of which structure we are functioning through, we can easily fall prey to operating in a counterfeit anointing through spirits of domination, manipulation, intimidation or emotional blackmail.

Chapter 5

ESTABLISHING A FOUNDATION

Vision is crucial to any work—we must see what we need to do. Vision is precision—perceiving exactly what God has released in the eternal realm and speaking the manifestation of its release into the earth. That is our goal in a supernatural work. To achieve this, we must establish a foundation for the supernatural. The foundation is built by prayer and fasting.

PRAYER

Prayer is our communication mechanism with God. Our primary goal in our Christian life is to fellowship with God. We must remain in communication with him; that interaction starts with prayer. As we meet with him in prayer, we receive the guidance and assurance that he is with us, and will give us our provision each day and in every circumstance.

If God has called us to a supernatural work, we will receive a prompting or unction from God in regard to our assignment. As we seek him in prayer, he brings revelation of what it is and what we are to do, and how we are to do it. It is God who reveals the strategy, pattern and protocol of what he is ordaining in this work. It is HIS WORK. We are the vessel(s) he is working through.

Walking in the Spirit

The scripture tells us to look to Jesus as the author and finisher of our faith (Hebrews 12:2). By acknowledging him in all our ways, he will direct our paths (Proverbs 3:6). We understand these scriptures intellectually, but what does it actually mean to walk in the Spirit?

According to God, it means choosing life over death. *"I call heaven and earth to record this day against you, that I have set before you life and death, blessing and cursing: therefore choose life, that both thou and thy seed may live"* (Deut. 30:19 KJV). It means moment-by-moment, we make choices that either bring life, or cause death.

To walk in the Spirit requires being filled with the Spirit. *And they were all filled with the Holy Ghost, and began to speak with other tongues, as the Spirit gave them utterance* (Acts 2:4 KJV). A supernatural work will necessitate that the full power of the Holy Spirit is accessible and operating fully in our lives. We need all the giftings and workings of the Spirit to fulfill our assignment, not least of which is using our gift of tongues to war in the Spirit against the enemy. Our part is to remain open in the situation; God, through his Spirit, will flow through us in the giftings needed for that particular circumstance.

Moreover, to walk in the Spirit, we must be Spirit-led. This means we are God-conscious in our choices. We pray each day and acknowledge God to set our day in order. Once we pray in faith, we then trust God to lead and guide us into the truth of that day. This allows us to move forward in peace. Because of this acknowledgment, no person or circumstance that confronts us can confound us. As we are assailed with problems or decisions during the day, we simply ask the Holy Spirit for guidance and counsel. God has promised in his Word, that in *everything*, we are more than a conqueror (Romans 8:37).

If we are God-conscious, we resist the temptation to fulfill the lusts of the flesh. These are graphically illustrated in Galatians 5:19-21 in the Message Bible:

It is obvious what kind of life develops out of trying to get your own way all the time: repetitive, loveless, cheap sex; a stinking accumulation of mental and emotional garbage; frenzied and joyless grabs for happiness; trinket gods; magic-show religion; paranoid loneliness; cutthroat competition; all-consuming-yet-never-satisfied wants; a brutal temper; an impotence to love or be loved; divided homes and divided lives; small-minded and lopsided pursuits; the vicious habit of depersonalizing everyone into a rival; uncontrolled and uncontrollable addictions; ugly parodies of community. I could go on. This isn't the first time I have warned you, you know. If you use your freedom this way, you will not inherit God's kingdom.

The flesh is ever-present to lead us into bondage and place us on the pathway of death. However, if we are God-conscious, we *choose* life. To choose life is to pick from the fruit of the Spirit from the tree of life. Therefore, we choose to initiate and respond to people and circumstances according to Galatians 5:22-24 (Message):

But what happens when we live God's way? He brings gifts into our lives, much the same way that fruit appears in an orchard – things like affection for others, exuberance about life, serenity. We develop willingness to stick with things, a sense of compassion in the heart, and a conviction that a basic holiness permeates things and people. We find ourselves involved in loyal commitments, not needing to force our way in life, able to marshal and direct our energies wisely. Legalism is helpless in bringing this about; it only gets in the way. Among those who belong to Christ, everything connected with getting our own way and mindlessly responding to what everyone else calls necessities is killed off for good – crucified.

God's Pattern Revealed

As we live and walk in the Spirit, God infuses into our Spirit the pattern of the work he has called us to build for his glory. For the pattern to evolve, we must spend time in his presence, in communion with his Spirit. He will reveal the pattern; he will provide the grid—the framework. *"When the Spirit of truth comes, he will guide you into all truth. He will not speak on his own but will tell you what he has heard. He will tell you about the future. He will bring me glory by telling you whatever he receives from me"* (John 16:13-14 NLT).

God works through divine structure. He has a pattern and a protocol designed in the heavenlies that he desires to manifest on earth. Our role is to receive the pattern and follow it exactly. Moses received the pattern of the tabernacle in communion with God on Mount Sinai. God does not bless or condone deviations to his divine pattern. *"Be sure that everything you make follows the pattern I am showing you here on the mountain"* (Exodus 25:40 NLT).

Our approach to following the Lord's direction should be the same as Joshua's as he prepared to fulfill his assignment to take the Promised Land. *When Joshua was near the town of Jericho, he looked up and saw a man standing in front of him with sword in hand. Joshua went up to him and demanded, "Are you friend or foe?" "Neither one," he replied. "I am the commander of the Lord's army." At this, Joshua fell with his face to the ground in reverence. "I am at your command," Joshua said. "What do you want your servant to do?"* (Joshua 5:13-15 NLT).

Promises and Prayer Strategies

As we establish communication with God, we become more in tune with his promises. While we commune with him in worship and prayer, promises in his Word become a *rhema* word or living — *now* word in our spirit. In each supernatural work, God gives us over-arching promises in his Word. We must *rest* on these promises *meaning we internalize them in our spirit so that we operate from that promise despite the situation or circumstances around us that reflect the opposite of what is promised.* This "rest" is the gestation period, that precipitates the crowning — the birthing of a supernatural work. The gestation period is the development timeframe between conception and the birth of an infant. God deposits into our spirit his divine blueprint during the gestation period; the plan and purpose is knit together in our spirit. As we rest on his promises, God is performing a work of his Spirit in us that will transform us internally to be a carrier of the supernatural realm. What we are carrying internally will manifest to perform what God has called us to do.

Abraham is a prime example of a believer called to a supernatural work, who continued believing *in faith* the promise — regardless of delays, mistakes, impossibilities and negative circumstances. In chapter 12 of the book of Genesis, God called Abraham to leave the land of his birth without giving him the location of his destination. God promised Abraham, who had no children because his wife was barren, that he would be the father of a great nation. This situation in the natural was set wholly in negative circumstances, contrary to the promise God had just given to Abraham. Departing from home and family, meant that Abraham was leaving all the connections and resources he had built up over a lifetime—everything physically required to build a nation! In order to believe he would be a father of nations, he must first believe that God could work through the barrenness of his wife Sarah, who was beyond the age of bearing children. To Abraham's credit, in faith he believed God's promise, although *all* the circumstances opposed the credibility of the promise's fulfillment.

While Abraham believed God's promise, he still made mistakes along the way; and so may we. However, if we rest in his promises, *he will bring them to pass*. God has assured us his goodness and mercy shall follow us (Psalm 23)—we are insulated with his goodness and mercy. Satan, our enemy, will attempt to derail us. He attempts to bring fear, doubt or a strategy that appears feasible to our human understanding. We must entrust ourselves, and the work, to the Lord's goodness and mercy; then move forward in faith. If we take a wrong turn in the process, God will ensure we get back onto the correct path. Notwithstanding, any deviation from God's plan will cause destruction in some form, which is why we must remain in a position of sensitivity to the Holy Spirit's prompting and guidance.

Abraham made the mistake of getting into the flesh to *make* the promise happen out of the Lord's timing, and in a way contrary to the Lord's. The result was Ishmael; a son Abraham dearly loved but who was not the son of the promise (Genesis 16). The Jews are still suffering the repercussions of this fleshly strategy. Ishmael became the father of the Arab nations that fight against Israel to this day. This scenario illustrates why it is so vital to stay attuned to the Holy Spirit in a supernatural work. We must believe, trust in, and adhere to the promises and the pattern (the way) God reveals to us *exactly*, without detours into the world's or our own ways of achieving the work.

God brought Abraham back on track. Nonetheless, he endured 13 years of silence before God spoke to him again and reconfirmed the promise. He instructed Abraham that the promise would be fulfilled through Sarah, his wife.

> *Then God said: "No, Sarah your wife shall bear you a son, and you shall call his name Isaac; I will establish My covenant with him for an everlasting covenant, and with his descendants after him. And as for Ishmael, I have*

heard you. Behold, I have blessed him, and will make him fruitful, and will multiply him exceedingly. He shall beget twelve princes, and I will make him a great nation. But My covenant I will establish with Isaac, whom Sarah shall bear to you at this set time next year" (Genesis 17:19-21 NKJV).

To stay the course without detours, derailing and deceptions is a monumental endeavor that is only possible through moment-by-moment guidance of the Holy Spirit. Fortunately, in our New Testament era, the way is opened to us, as the Holy Spirit resides *inside* of us. Abraham could only experience infrequent visitations of the Spirit coming upon him, while we may walk in the continuous flow of the Holy Spirit. Despite the Holy Spirit's indwelling, we must choose to follow the promptings and leadings of his still, small voice. To ignore him may prove quite costly, and result in silence, if we are disobedient to our last instruction. Whenever the *heavens seem as brass*, our first response should be to retreat to our prayer closet.

Patterns of Prayer

Prayer is communication, our way of talking to God. There are different forms of communication with him just as we engage in different forms of communication with those around us in the earthly realm.

1. **Repentance**

    This is the *only* prayer God will hear if we have sinned. We come to him with a contrite heart acknowledging our specific sin, and asking him to forgive and extend us his mercy. In a supernatural work, we have no previous roadmap; God is taking us into new and uncharted territory. We will make mistakes. When we do, we repent and forgive ourselves as he has forgiven us—and move on as Paul did. *"I don't mean to say that I have already achieved these things or that I have already reached perfection. But I press on to possess that perfection for which Christ Jesus first possessed me. No, dear brothers and sisters, I have not achieved it but I focus on this one thing: Forgetting the past and looking forward to what lies ahead"* (Philippians 3:11-13 NLT).

2. **Adoration and Thankfulness**

    Adoration: Prayers of love, adoration or worship, express our love for him and praise the greatness of God. We acknowledge our dependence upon him and recognize he is both the source and object of all love. If we truly love him, we spend time in his presence, not to ask for things from his hand, but to rejoice and treasure being the object of his love.

Thankfulness: One of the most neglected types of prayer is prayer of thanksgiving. Thankfulness is the gateway into the Lord's presence. *Enter into His gates with thanksgiving, And into His courts with praise. Be thankful to Him, and bless His name* (Psalm 100:4 NKJV). A thankful heart forms an attitude of gratitude that responds with grace to life's challenges. Rather than react to people and circumstances, thankfulness allows us to enter into the Lord's rest, where the Holy Spirit will guides us to speak and act appropriately in each encounter throughout our day. As we form the habit of thanking God in everything that happens to us, and for each person that crosses our path, we will walk in increased *peace* because we are operating from a place of *rest*, even in the midst of great turmoil or instability. Most importantly, we should thank him for each answered prayer. This not only keeps us in the attitude of gratitude, it reminds us of what God has done, and is continuing to do—great works in and through us!

Prayers of adoration and thankfulness should be an integral part of our communication with God. This type of prayer places us in a posture of worship that opens the gates of heaven to us.

3. Petition

Prayers of petition are the most frequent and familiar type of prayer we, as believers, engage in. Philippians 4:6-7 (NLT) illustrates this form of prayer. *Don't worry about anything; instead, pray about everything. Tell God what you need, and thank him for all he has done. Then you will experience God's peace, which exceeds anything we can understand. His peace will guard your hearts and minds as you live in Christ Jesus.* As the Holy Spirit leads us in a supernatural work, we ask God for the things we need both physically and spiritually. Sometimes we do not know in the natural what is needed with a particular person or situation. At these times, we must pray in the Spirit. *Likewise the Spirit also helps in our weaknesses. For we do not know what we should pray for as we ought, but the Spirit Himself makes intercession for us with groanings which cannot be uttered* (Romans 8:26 NKJV). The Holy Spirit will pray through us what is the will of the Father.

The point of all prayer of petition is to pray in the will of God, not our emotions or our own desires. We must truly be seeking his will with the person or the situation, not what we want or what would lead to the path of least resistance. The outcome of prayers of petition is that his will, his purpose and his plan be fulfilled.

As with all relationships, intimacy deepens the more honest and open we are with each other. Prayers of petition keep us connected with God on a daily basis.

4. Intercessory

Intercessory prayer is praying on behalf of others. There are times and seasons in a supernatural work in which it is not appropriate to confront an issue or a person head-on. Rather, God would have us to intercede for what he has revealed to us but not to others. This serves two purposes. First it crucifies our flesh and humbles us. We may be the vessel God is using anonymously to change a heart or situation; however, we may not be the vessel chosen to reap the benefits of our intercession—meaning someone else may get the credit or that person/situation may be in rebellion, and therefore, will not result in a kingdom decision.

Secondly, intercession is preparatory in that the Holy Spirit prompts, tills the soil, and speaks to the heart of the person or situation so that they are prepared to receive the message, correction, or change in direction or attitude.

True intercessory prayer is characterized by fervency, self-denial, confession, unselfish identification with the person/situation and is dependent on God's character. The goal of all intercessory prayer is God's glory. We are to come to God on behalf of others and situations with a heartbroken and repentant attitude. We recognize our own unworthiness—not standing on our own righteousness, or right to demand anything from God. Rather, we identify ourselves as part of the problem, and confess our sin. Our desire is to see God's will fulfilled whether it benefits us or not, and at whatever cost to us personally.

5. Commanding

Commanding prayer is based on faith and standing in our authority in Christ. The premise of commanding prayer is that *we have what we speak* whether positive or negative. Therefore, we speak, decree and declare the promises of God over our lives and situations. The goal of commanding prayer is to bring what we speak into alignment with the Word of God, and appropriate the authority of Christ, so that we are blessing our lives and not cursing them by the words of our mouth. *And Jesus said unto them, Because of your unbelief: for verily I say unto you, If ye have faith as a grain of mustard seed, ye shall **say** unto this mountain, Remove hence to yonder place; and it shall remove; and nothing shall be impossible unto you* (Matthew 17:20 KJV, emphasis added).

Three elements are essential for effective commanding prayer. First, we must have a promise in the Word, or a rhema (revealed) Word from God (that aligns with scripture) concerning the person or situation. Second, we must *believe in our heart* what we are speaking. The Word of God is not magic; it is activated through *faith*—we must truly believe—this *sets in motion* the Word. God says his Word will not return void; it will accomplish the purpose for which it was sent (Isaiah 55:11). Third, we must know in our heart *we have the authority* in Christ to speak into a situation. We are children of the King and co-heirs with Christ. Jesus assured us, *Behold, I give you the **authority** to trample on serpents and scorpions, and over **all** the power of the enemy, and nothing shall by any means hurt you* (Luke 10:19 NKJV, emphasis added).

6. Soaking

Soaking prayer is simply resting in the Lord's love. We come before him without an agenda or request. We are present to him. Our thoughts and Spirit are focused on ministering to his heart. This is the highest form of prayer and is the desire of God's heart. *As they **ministered to** the Lord and fasted, the Holy Spirit said, "Now separate to Me Barnabas and Saul for the work to which I have called them"* (Acts 13:2 NKJV, emphasis added). In soaking, we surrender to the Holy Spirit, to whatever he wants to do or speak. We quiet our Spirit and wait before the Lord, as his priest, offering our hearts on the altar of sacrifice.

In many instances in times of soaking, individuals experience a divine encounter such as being transported in Spirit to the third heaven, or an open vision in which God sheds light on a situation or relationship bringing revelation, clarity, direction or instruction.

A biblical example of an open vision in which all these elements were present is recorded in Acts 10:1-20 NKJV).

> *The next day, as they went on their journey and drew near the city, Peter went up on the housetop to pray, about the sixth hour. Then he became very hungry and wanted to eat; but while they made ready, he fell into a trance and saw heaven opened and an object like a great sheet bound at the four corners, descending to him and let down to the earth. In it were all kinds of four-footed animals of the earth, wild beasts, creeping things, and birds of the air. And a voice came to him, "Rise, Peter; kill and eat."*
>
> *But Peter said, "Not so, Lord! For I have never eaten anything common or unclean." And a voice spoke to him again the second time, "What God has cleansed you must not call common." This was done three times. And the object was taken up into heaven again. Now while Peter wondered within himself what this vision which he had seen meant, behold, the men who had been sent from Cornelius had made inquiry for Simon's house, and stood before the gate. And they called and asked whether Simon, whose surname was Peter, was lodging there.*
>
> *While Peter thought about the vision, the Spirit said to him, "Behold, three men are seeking you. Arise therefore, go down and go with them, doubting nothing; for I have sent them."*

Soaking is a type of prayer that deepens our relationship with the Lord; soaking seats us in heavenly places to see and hear what he is doing. Then, as we encounter obstacles, hindrances, issues in relationships and circumstances, his presence within us has already encountered the situation or person, and the path is illumined to our Spirit, not our mind. We remain in-step with the Holy Spirit, not blown off course by each adverse wind.

7. **Warfare**

Warfare prayer is a form of intense spiritual battle against the kingdom of darkness. God calls us to be warriors in his Kingdom. Lack of understanding of spiritual warfare has caused many supernatural works to falter. We will outline the mechanics of this form of prayer in detail in Chapter 12. Ephesians 6:12 (NLT) identifies who we are actually fighting as we engage in spiritual warfare. *For we are not fighting against people made of flesh and blood, but against persons without bodies – the evil rulers of the unseen world, those mighty satanic beings and great evil princess of darkness who rule this world; and against huge numbers of wicked spirits in the spirit world.* Warfare prayer requires an intense focus on the leading of the Holy Spirit, acknowledging the supremacy of our Lord, and taking over the atmosphere in his Name. This form of prayer is a combination of praise, intercession and decreeing the Word of God into the atmosphere. It is most effective when supported by fasting.

FASTING

Some things only come out through fasting and prayer (Matthew 17:14-21 NKJV). Not only is that true in deliverance, but it also applies to a supernatural work of God. A supernatural work of God is a target of the enemy. Before Jesus started his supernatural work on earth, he fasted and prayed in the desert for 40 days. He sustained himself with the Word of God.

When we fast and pray, we must commit our way unto the Lord and he will bring it to pass (Psalms 37:5). The seventh verse of Psalm 37 instructs us to rest in the Lord and wait patiently for him. Don't get ahead of him, or behind what he is doing. Our willingness to deny our flesh, and seek the Spirit wholeheartedly, pleases the Lord. It demonstrates we are more concerned about our assignment than our physical comfort.

Combined with prayer and worship, fasting is a powerful tool. What happens as we fast is that our bodily functions are subdued and our Spirit man rises and comes to the forefront. We become more sensitive to his voice and his promptings. The clogs of our desires, wants and needs are flushed out and the conduit to our Spirit is opened; God can then initiate a Spirit-to-Spirit flow. Revelation knowledge and divine plans and purposes flow into our Spirit. What we receive in this flow might have taken months or years to learn through study; however, a Holy Spirit download can impart into our Spirit knowledge, wisdom, discernment and the counsel we need instantaneously!

Spiritual Warfare

Fasting heightens our effectiveness in spiritual warfare. The mechanics of this form of prayer are outlined in specific detail in chapter 12, *Charge and Change the Atmosphere*. A supernatural work is a battle. Satan loves works of the flesh as they offer no long-term hindrance to his kingdom—they have no eternal value and will be burned up on the Day of Judgment (1 Cor. 3:15). A supernatural work, ordained of God and carried out through the work of the Holy Spirit, is another matter. This work will have eternal impact that will tear down the works of Satan (I John 3:8). These are the works that Satan himself comes against, rather than delegating the work of destruction to his demonic minions. Every time he and his works are exposed, it shortens his time on earth to rob, kill and destroy before he is thrown into the pit. *Therefore rejoice, ye heavens, and ye that dwell in them. Woe to the inhabiters of the earth and of the sea! for the devil is come down unto you, having great wrath, because he knoweth that he hath but a short time* (Revelation 12:12 KJV).

Satan reacts with great wrath to a divine work of God. A supernatural work will manifest the light and authority of God's kingdom upon the earth, diminishing Satan's rule and exposing the darkness—the cover under which he operates to deceive and control undetected. Therefore, Satan pits himself against a supernatural work, throwing his entire arsenal of darkness against it.

We cannot fight Satan in the flesh. He is a mighty archangel of superior intelligence. Consequently, our weapons cannot be carnal (man's reasoning) but mighty (spiritual) to the tearing down of Satan's strongholds. *For the **weapons** of our warfare are **not carnal**, but mighty through God to the pulling down of strong holds* (2 Cor. 10:4 KJV, emphasis added).

An effective strategy to pull down Satan's strongholds is to fast and engage in warfare prayer. Warfare prayer is prayer directed at exposing the demonic root that would, or is hindering, a supernatural work of God.

A number of years ago I (Jan) was led by the Lord to start a women's Bible study with a Christian friend. As the Bible study matured, the Lord led us to combine the Bible study with a retreat. The Lord would give us the theme of the retreat. From the date we set the retreat, we fasted and prayed for direction, the teachings, and most importantly, the presence and work of the Holy Spirit amongst us. The first couple of retreats were held without incident and we began to witness a deep move of the Spirit resulting in dramatic changes in individual walks with the Lord.

The retreats were held at a mountain ski lodge; we felt the manifest presence of God setting his throne on the mountain for the duration of the retreat. Many experienced powerful deliverances, healings and prophetic words. Each retreat would bring a deeper level of healing, deliverance and restoration, as God ministered to us and we to him, under an *open heaven*. Notwithstanding, we began to experience Satanic attack. Initially, he attacked individuals, including leaders, with sickness at the retreat. We became wise to this tactic and proactively fasted, prayed and decreed divine health over the retreat.

Additionally, Satan would attack us through the weather—snowstorms, extreme cold, rain, thunder and lightning—depending on the season. Here again, I began to take authority over the weather and decree sunshine and a comfortable seasonal temperature. I had read in chapter 10 of the book of Joshua that during a battle he spoke to the sun and the moon to stay in their places. In other words, he took authority over the cessation of light and the advent of darkness—changing the length of earth's day. He exercised authority over heavenly bodies! Surely, if God granted this level of authority to Joshua before Jesus won back our dominion over the earth from the devil, I could speak to the weather forecast! I did and the volatile weather would cease, or only rain while we were in session and clear up during our free time.

It is interesting that during a session in which a prophet was speaking about receiving holy words from God's throne, a thunder and lightning storm ensued and God punctuated divine truths with thunder—his voice from his throne! God physically manifested through the weather.

After these initial attempts to hinder the retreats were thwarted, Satan became more insidious and devious in his strategy to infiltrate and hinder the work God was doing amongst us. We had a group of two to four individuals leading the retreats—creating the agenda, teaching, physically organizing and praying. We began experiencing problems within the leadership. During worship we prayed and came against the works of Satan. However, things worsened. In desperation, I cried out to the Lord to reveal the root of the problem. A member of the Bible study approached me with a dream she believed was prophetic. In the dream, she had seen snakes crawling and attempting to bite people. I was greatly disturbed; I knew in my spirit God was communicating a warning and I sought the Lord for clarity of the spiritual entity.

A few days before the scheduled retreat, during my prayer time, the Lord gave me Isaiah 27:1 (KJV) *In that day the LORD with his sore and great and strong sword shall punish leviathan the piercing serpent, even leviathan that crooked serpent; and he shall slay the dragon that is in the sea.*

In God's perfect timetable, I had watched a ministry program by Pastor Ron Phillips discussing his book *Everyone's Guide to Demons and Spiritual Warfare.*[1] I immediately went to the Internet and ordered this book. Amazingly, it arrived a day and a half later—two days before the retreat. The book contained a section on Leviathan. Phillips identified this spirit as the number one enemy in the church. Leviathan is a coiling serpent which tries to hide where God's Word and the Spirit are flowing among believers. This spirit twists the truth and refuses to live in covenant. Therefore, when someone is infected with this spirit, he or she will create division and destroy covenant relationships. Leviathan hides underneath the water and remains hidden until exposed by God.

God had exposed the spirit; although we, as a leadership group, prayed against it, we did not have an offensive strategy to oppose this spirit. We simply urged the women to extend grace to one another, as the Lord had revealed the enemy was going to try to create strife and offense. Because we had experienced problems within the leadership, this spirit found an opening at the retreat. Fighting the good fight of spiritual warfare is a learning process and our leadership was taken through the purifying learning fire.

At the retreat, our leadership team made the mistake of not addressing the issues immediately with the one leader who had not fulfilled her responsibilities prior to the retreat, and then expected to fulfill her designated leadership accountability at the retreat. This opened the door for Leviathan; he entered through a most unexpected door—food!

Several of the women followed strict natural food diets and Leviathan weaseled in twisting words to bring offense. His goal was to break covenant relationships. God revealed and convicted the individual leaders to address the issue with the offended leader. Our objective was to restore unity of the Spirit in the leadership group. We, as a leadership group, met in private and apologized to the offended leader for not addressing the issue sooner, and for the offense we had caused. Sadly, this did not restore full unity of the group. However, the remaining leaders committed to stay in unity as we discerned what Leviathan was attempting to do and was succeeding in—bringing offense to break relationships and destroy the work of the Holy Spirit at the retreat!

The leaders addressed the "food offense" with all the retreat participants. Those of us who had spoken carelessly, but without intent to harm, apologized; we asked forgiveness from those offended. This act of repentance honored God and maintained the authority of the Holy Spirit over the retreat. Throughout the week, the Holy Spirit brought those whose hearts were open and willing, to deep places of spiritual renewal and deliverance. All the while, Leviathan was attempting to create havoc and chaos!

Post-retreat, the leadership met and realized that Leviathan had indeed inflicted damage to covenant relationships. Again, we attempted to restore relationships. Subsequent to this retreat which was held in the Fall, we determined to seek the Lord for an offensive strategy against Leviathan for the Spring retreat. Our desire was to do battle in the heavenlies prior to the retreat, and not be in a position of employing a defensive strategy against this spirit during the Spring retreat. We had been warned again in a dream of one of our Bible study members, and a vision by one of the leaders that Leviathan would attack again.

Our leadership group designated each Monday as a fast day. We met on scheduled Monday's throughout the winter and organized a pre-retreat meeting to strategize, pray and worship. In one of these sessions, a member of the leadership team saw a vision of a huge snake. God was warning us that Leviathan sought entrance again. At this juncture, we had learned we could not just pray against this spirit to bind it and take authority over it; we needed an offensive strategy to subdue it. We sought the Lord in prayer.

The Lord answered through a book, by Geri Keller, *Father: A search Into the Heart of God.*[2] Pastor and author Geri Keller spoke of the church as a giant liver, cleansing the body of Christ of toxic substances like rumors, slander and pain. These substances circulate as poisons in the body. As believers, it is our accountability to come to the altar and burn what needs to be burnt in the fire of our prayers. This detoxifies the body of Christ from these circulating poisons. We had the answer! Using the text, we wrote *a Vow of Purity* that each woman at the retreat would recite. This vow would be part of the opening ceremony of the retreat. The ceremony involved a large frankincense candle (representing our vow wafting up to God as incense). The frankincense candle was lit and each participant was given a myrrh-scented votive candle. Each woman took her votive candle and lit it from the frankincense candle and made this vow of purity before the Lord.

> **My Vow of Purity**
> Purify my lips! Help me to be a priestly believer! I want to be Your priest, oh God! What else do I need to do? I will not spread anything negative about the other believers in attendance while here or after the retreat. If a believer is not doing well, I will take their pain and burden to God in prayer. It is not an option to spread the news. Rather, it is an opportunity for me to bless that person, to encourage and comfort her and to help rebuild what is broken. I vow to be a river of living water at this retreat, not a stopped-up well.

This offensive strategy worked beautifully. Leviathan's tactics were successfully counteracted and we experienced the most peaceful and harmonious retreat ever! At the retreat wrap-up session, a majority of the women commented that the *Vow of Purity* had been a highlight of the retreat and a constant reminder to walk in grace.

As we are apprenticed under the Master Builder, the various forms of prayer outlined in this chapter become vehicles to communicate with the Master. When our prayer life is combined with fasting, it signals our determination to deny our flesh and pursue the Father's will with single-heartedness. It puts the heavenly realm on alert and thwarts the demonic realm. The intimacy we build with him in our times of communion, keeps us in right alignment with heaven and the blueprint we have received. In prayer, we are plugged into God's heart. It is both our most effective tool and greatest weapon to execute "exactly" the Master's plan.

Chapter 6

GOD'S GOVERNMENTAL STRUCTURE

The greatest pitfall to a supernatural work is to align it according to the government of the world, rather than the government of the kingdom. As stated in Isaiah 9:6 (KJV), the government of God is embodied in Christ. *For unto us a child is born, unto us a son is given: and the government shall be upon his shoulder: and his name shall be called Wonderful, Counsellor, The mighty God, The everlasting Father, The Prince of Peace.* Our goal as believers is to bring the Kingdom of God to earth—that is *his* rule according to *his* government. When we align the work according to the government of the kingdom, all the attributes of that government permeate the work. We have access to divine counsel that is wiser than the world and our spiritual enemies. He empowers us and the work with his might—the dunamis—resurrection power that overpowers all opposition and infuses it with the glory realm. It is in the glory that miracles, signs and wonders manifest. Our mantle and anointing flow through his might. The everlasting Father watches over the work performing his Word through it. It manifests as an eternal work that will not burn up at the Judgment seat as wood, hay, or stubble.

The peace of God rules over it—the unity of the Spirit that allows the people and the work to function in one accord.

All rule in the Kingdom of God flows from his throne. This is why God's throne must be established in our heart, before we can lead a supernatural work. The throne of God ruling inside us provides the foundation to understand God's throne from a governmental ruling perspective.

THE STRUCTURE OF GOD'S THRONE

The foundation of God's throne is righteousness and justice (Psalm 97:2). The fourth chapter of the book of Revelation gives an awe-inspiring picture of God's throne room in heaven.

> *Then immediately I was in the Spirit; and behold, a throne set in heaven, and One sat on the throne. And He who sat there was like a jasper and a sardius stone in appearance; and there was a rainbow around the throne, in appearance like an emerald. Around the throne were twenty-four thrones, and on the thrones I saw twenty-four elders sitting, clothed in white robes; and they had crowns of gold on their heads. And from the throne proceeded lightnings, thunderings, and voices. Seven lamps of fire were burning before the throne, which are the seven Spirits of God.*

> *Before the throne there was a sea of glass, like crystal. And in the midst of the throne, and around the throne, were four living creatures full of eyes in front and in back. The first living creature was like a lion, the second living creature like a calf, the third living creature had a face like a man, and the fourth living creature was like a flying eagle. The four living creatures, each having six wings, were full of eyes around and within. And they do not rest day or night, saying:*

> Holy, holy, holy,
> Lord God Almighty,
> Who was and is and is to come!"

Whenever the living creatures give glory and honor and thanks to Him who sits on the throne, who lives forever and ever, the twenty-four elders fall down before Him who sits on the throne and worship Him who lives forever and ever, and cast their crowns before the throne, saying:

"You are worthy, O Lord,
To receive glory and honor and power;
For You created all things,
And by Your will they exist and were created" (Revelation 4:2-11 NKJV).

In his wisdom, God provided this majestic glimpse of the heavenly throne room. Every description in God's Word serves a divine purpose. Christ reveals the structure of the heavenly court. The Father's throne is central in the heavenly court room. The throne is encircled with an emerald-like rainbow, which signifies his promises which cannot be broken and are ever before him. Before the throne is a sea of crystal, meaning everything is transparent before the throne of God; nothing is hidden so that his judgments are both righteous and holy because they are based on true justice. Justice is his kingship in establishing and maintaining what is *right* as defined by his nature. God is not indifferent to good and evil as Habakkuk 1:13 (AMP) illustrates. *You are of purer eyes than to behold evil and can not look [inactively] upon injustice. Why then do You look upon the plunderer? Why are you silent when the wicked one destroys him who is more righteous than [the Chaldean oppressor] is?*

At times, we respond similarly to Habakkuk when we perceive God as silent or inactive in terms of judging unrighteousness. However, God *is* justice; he embodies the concept, while our understanding and perspective is limited; therefore, we must uphold God's nature, rather than cling to our *sense* of justice in a particular situation.

His throne, where Christ is seated at his right hand, is surrounded by 24 thrones upon which the elders sit as is described in greater detail in Revelation 5:1-12 (NKJV):

And I saw in the right hand of Him who sat on the throne a scroll written inside and on the back, sealed with seven seals. Then I saw a strong angel proclaiming with a loud voice, "Who is worthy to open the scroll and to loose its seals?" And no one in heaven or on the earth or under the earth was able to open the scroll, or to look at it.

So I wept much, because no one was found worthy to open and read the scroll, or to look at it. But one of the elders said to me, "Do not weep. Behold, the Lion of the tribe of Judah, the Root of David, has prevailed to open the scroll and to loose its seven seals."

And I looked, and behold, in the midst of the throne and of the four living creatures, and in the midst of the elders, stood a Lamb as though it had been slain, having seven horns and seven eyes, which are the seven Spirits of God sent out into all the earth. Then He came and took the scroll out of the right hand of Him who sat on the throne.

Now when He had taken the scroll, the four living creatures and the twenty-four elders fell down before the Lamb, each having a harp, and golden bowls full of incense, which are the prayers of the saints.

"You are worthy to take the scroll, And to open its seals; For You were slain,

And have redeemed us to God by Your blood Out of every tribe and tongue and people and nation, And have made us kings and priests to our God; And we shall reign on the earth."

Then I looked, and I heard the voice of many angels around the throne, the living creatures, and the elders; and the number of them was ten thousand times ten thousand, and thousands of thousands, saying with a loud voice: "Worthy is the Lamb who was slain To receive power and riches and wisdom, And strength and honor and glory and blessing!"

In the midst of the throne are four living creatures. These creatures are referred to as Cherubim in the books of Genesis, Exodus and Ezekiel. In Genesis, God sent them to guard the tree of life. Interestingly, God could have chosen regular angels but Lucifer was a Cherub. These angels were of the rank of the heavenly host that is continuously in the presence of

God. Therefore, they possessed the authority of God's throne to keep Satan, as well as Adam and Eve, out of the garden (Genesis 3:23).

In Ezekiel, the Cherubim transport the heavenly throne to wherever God is judging in the earth (Ezekiel 1:1-12). In Exodus 25:20 (NKJV) they cover the mercy seat of the Ark of the Covenant in the earthly tabernacle of God. *And the cherubim shall stretch out their wings above, covering the mercy seat with their wings, and they shall face one another; the faces of the cherubim shall be toward the mercy seat.* The living creatures always surround the throne of God. They travel with and transport the throne wherever God executes his justice in heaven and earth.

The Holy Spirit, his full attributes — the seven Spirits — the *Spirit upon, wisdom and understanding, counsel and might, knowledge and fear of the Lord*, flow from the throne (Isaiah 11:2). "*The testimony of Jesus is the spirit of prophecy*" (Revelation 19:10 NKJV). Christ issues revelation of himself and what is to come to believers through the attributes of the Holy Spirit. The Godhead operates in unity — in oneness.

The twenty-four elders surround the throne of God. In scholarly circles their identity has spawned much debate. However, the earthly temple of Solomon was patterned after the heavenly temple. "*And see to it that you make them according to the pattern which was shown you on the mountain*" (Exodus 25:40 NKJV). The earthly temple had rotations of 24 Levitical priests to minister before the Lord patterning the 24 elders ministering to the Lord before the heavenly throne (I Chronicles 24:19). The elders are the heavenly priestly order.

The throne of God is structured around worship. Wafting as incense before the throne are the heavenly music of the living creatures and the prayers of the saints. All heaven is submitted to the throne. The elders cast their crowns before the Father and Son bowing down in worship. The elders crowns are not diadem or rulers' crowns; rather they are *stephanos* — the crown of the *overcomer*. This is the same crown described in James 1:12 (NKJV) that faithful believers will receive at the Judgment Seat of Christ. *Blessed [is] the man who endures temptation; for when he has been approved, he will receive the crown of life which the Lord has promised to those who love Him.*

Psalm 50:2-6 (NLT) further describes the Father on his throne in judgment.

From Mount Zion, the perfection of beauty, God shines in glorious radiance. Our God approaches, and he is not silent. Fire devours everything in his way, and a great storm rages around him. He calls on the heavens above and earth below to witness the judgment of his people. "Bring my faithful people to me – those who made a covenant with me by giving sacrifices." Then let the heavens proclaim his justice, for God himself will be the judge.

The atmosphere around the throne is stormy – lightning flashes and his voice thunders. God, himself, is a consuming fire (Deut.9:3; Psalm 97:3-4; Job 37:5; Exodus 24:17; Isaiah 33:14; Hebrews 12:29).

This is not a description of a democratic court, rather the court of a kingdom that is above all earthly rule issuing proclamations, declarations and judgments of celestial truths. These truths are immovable – they stand forever and are absolute. All is done in worship to bring glory to the King. This is the structure of government of a supernatural work.

SUPERNATURAL WORK STRUCTURE

The heavenly pattern and the earthly pattern of the throne of God form the structural framework for a supernatural work. This model is supported by two groups – elders/cherubs (heavenly throne); Aaronic priests/Levites (earthly pattern). These are the pillars that sustain the work. The elders (heavenly priests), and the Aaronic priests of the Old Covenant tabernacle, ministered to the Lord – through worship, decree and proclamation with the divine authority of the throne. The cherubs and Levites functioned in an administrative capacity to support and carry out that authority.

The formation of the government of the church followed this same pattern. The apostles and elders walked in governmental authority. They focused on worship and ministry of the Word, while the deacons were in charge of the administrative aspects of serving and carrying out that authority. Although we are no longer under the Levitical priesthood, the pattern of the priesthood remains. Through the apostle Peter the Lord affirmed, *But you are a chosen generation, a **royal priesthood**, a holy nation, His own special people, that you may proclaim the praises of Him who called you out of darkness into His marvelous light* (1 Peter 2:9 NKJV, emphasis added).

The apostle Paul instructed New Testament believers in their function as priests, *For He testifies: "You are a priest forever according to the order of Melchizedek"* (Hebrews 7:17 NKJV). In this New Testament priesthood, Jesus is our High Priest. *...where the forerunner has entered for us, even Jesus, having become High Priest forever according to the order of Melchizedek* (Hebrews 6:20 NKJV). God has not changed his pattern. He has transferred the priesthood from a fleshly Aaronic order, to a spiritual order of Melchizedek, with Christ as our High Priest.

The pattern was extended to every believer by the birth, life, death, and resurrection of Jesus Christ, the Anointed One, the Son of God, our Redeemer, Advocate, and High Priest. After Christ's death, the veil in the temple was rent (torn, split) which was symbolic of removing the old process—the laws/Adamic Sin that separated man from God. Christ's blood sacrifice and atonement provided mankind a way back into fellowship and direct communication with God through Christ who sent his Spirit—the Holy Spirit to us on the day of Pentecost.

We are now the redeemed sons and daughters of God—joint-heirs with Christ, kings and priests before God. This redeemed status becomes a reality in each of our lives when we confess our sins and are baptized in Jesus name. We receive the Holy Spirit as our guide, and begin living a sanctified life by faith—serving God with our entire mind, body, soul, and spirit. We serve him by faith. As we read and study his Word, our mind (thoughts) and actions come into compliance with our new status of blood-washed and blood-purchased children of God (Romans 8:1-14).

Elders and Deacons

Elders are the spiritual undergirding and function to build the foundation of the work. They have authority and accountability over *all* areas of the work. The Elders main objective is to create the environment that imparts unity of the Spirit, so that work and the people operate in one accord with the mind of Christ. They function to guide and assist others in internalizing the vision. Requirements to function as an elder include: maturity in the faith; the anointing of the seven-fold Holy Spirit and evidence of spiritual fruit that remains.

Deacons represent the administrative, hands-on, delegated authority of the work. As they have internalized the vision, they function as practical movers—carrying the mission to completion. They function to keep the work on-track and enforce the governmental authority of the elders. They operate with authority over specific areas of the work, in collaboration with all deacons to keep the work in alignment and progressing toward the goal.

These two groups form the framework. Other terms can be used as long as the authority and accountability structure follow the pattern of an *elder* and a *deacon*. In this book, we refer to them as governing leaders (i.e., master builder, deliverer/forerunner) and co-laboring leaders. This structure is not hierarchical in nature; rather it is a co-laborer structure that functions by anointed, delegated authority from the throne.

RULING FROM GOD'S THRONE

The foundation of a supernatural work is governed from the throne of God. God establishes us in his government and implements his government through us. The following illustration is a visual depiction of the elements of ruling from God's throne.

Righteousness and justice are the foundation of God's throne. They operate in tandem to bring his glory upon the earth. The purpose of righteousness is to align all things to the designs and purposes of God, while judgment (justice) sentences all that is in opposition to the throne. When these foundations pervade a work, God's enemies are displaced and put under his feet. His presence brings his will into our midst.

Our role as governmental leaders in the kingdom is to establish his celestial truths making them evident in the structure and the people. Celestial truths are biblical commands such as our commandment to love one another (John 13:34). They are represented in the 10 commandments that guide our relationship with God and our fellow man. Celestial truths are founded upon immovable and immutable laws and principles that govern the Kingdom of God. For example, the *principle of reciprocity* is an immutable law of *judging* in the kingdom. It is no respecter of persons; it states, *Give, and it shall be given unto you; good measure, pressed down, and shaken together, and running over, shall men give into your bosom. For with the same measure that ye mete withal it shall be measured to you again* (Luke 6:38 KJV). The context of these verses in Luke deal with judging others. The measure of your condemnation or forgiveness of others will be the same measurement used to judge you.

Celestial truths also represent God established patterns and protocols such as God's pattern and protocol for worship. The pattern is that we worship him in Spirit and in Truth (John 4:24); the protocol is: 1) that we enter through the gates of thanksgiving; 2) progress through the outer court of cleansing: 3) enter into the inner court of praise; and 4) move into the holy place of complete surrender to, and adoration of, the King (following the pattern of the Temple—Psalm 100:4).

The epilogue of this book, *Concepts in Practice* provides concrete examples of how to implement the throne of God into the organization. These concepts are established when they are immovable and visible in the lives of people and the structure. In this way, all things that pertain to the kingdom—resources, blessing, favor, etc., are attracted toward the throne of God that has been established in the people and the structure.

THE HEAVENLY THRONE

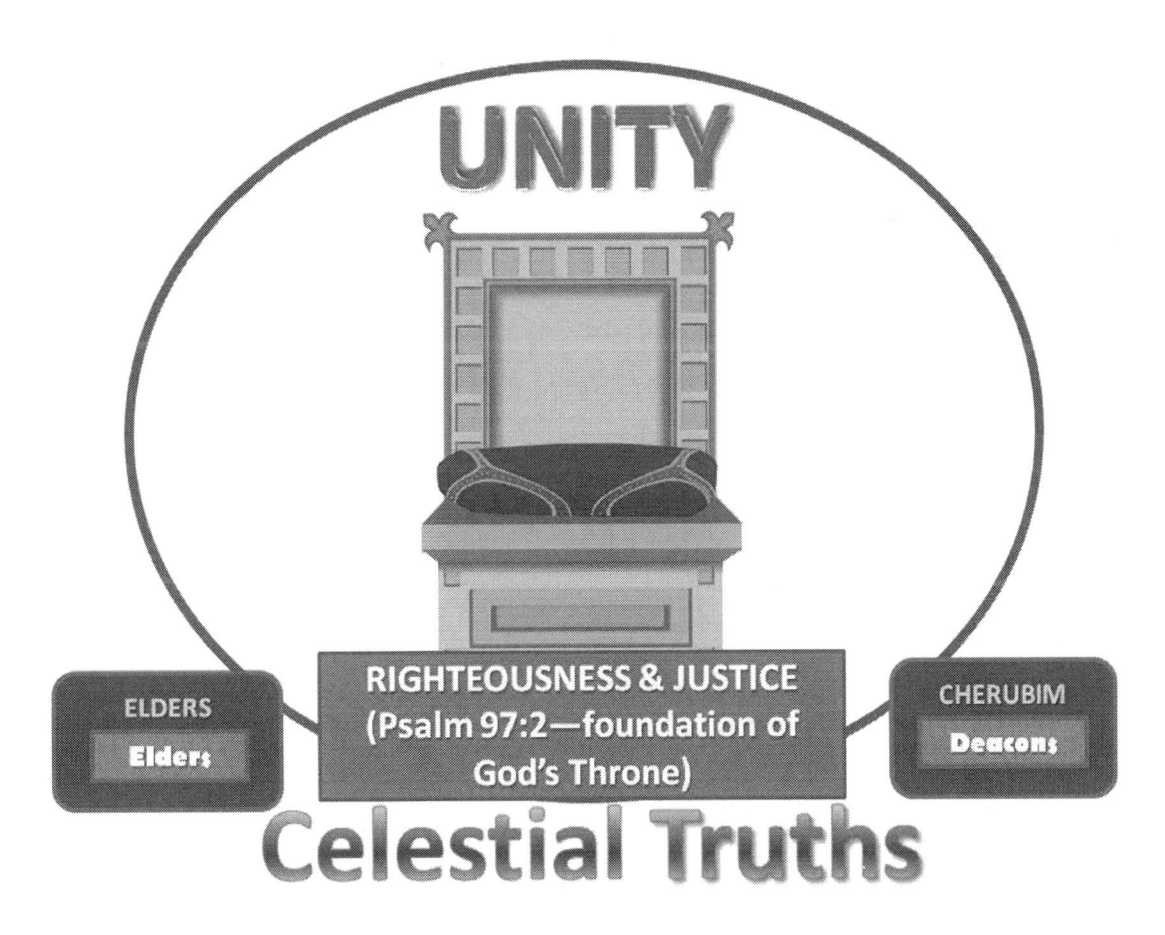

UNITY

ELDERS
Elders

RIGHTEOUSNESS & JUSTICE
(Psalm 97:2—foundation of God's Throne)

CHERUBIM
Deacons

Celestial Truths

Chapter 7

THE LEADER: DELIVERER AND FORERUNNER

Leadership in a supernatural work requires a deliverer and forerunner. We are so conditioned to implement programs in the body of Christ that we fail to understand that God is in the business of transformation and establishing his government in the earth. Both of these require leadership beyond the parameters of creating and implementing projects, schedules, and timelines. A supernatural work has a divine purpose that cannot be accomplished through mere human abilities and leadership skills.

God has ordained his works from the foundation of the world. In the book of Hebrews, Paul writes that God decreed the Israelites would not enter into his rest *"although the works were finished from the foundation of the world"* (Hebrews 4:3 NKJV). In each work, God anoints a chosen vessel or vessels to accomplish the work. The work can *only* be accomplished through entering his rest. This is the place of surrender where God's chosen vessel ceases from his or her own labors, reasoning and striving, and allows the Lord to prepare him/her to be a deliverer and forerunner.

Therefore, since a promise remains of entering His rest, let us fear lest any of you seem to have come short of it. For indeed the gospel was preached to us as well as to them; but the word which they heard did not profit them, not being mixed with faith in those who heard it. For we who have believed do enter that rest, as He has said: "So I swore in My wrath, 'They shall not enter My rest,' "although the works were finished from the foundation of the world. For He has spoken in a certain place of the seventh day in this way: "And God rested on the seventh day from all His works"; and again in this place: "They shall not enter My rest." Since therefore it remains that some must enter it, and those to whom it was first preached did not enter because of disobedience, again He designates a certain day, saying in David, "Today," after such a long time, as it has been said: "Today, if you will hear His voice, Do not harden your hearts." For if Joshua had given them rest, then He would not afterward have spoken of another day. There remains therefore a rest for the people of God. For he who has entered His rest has himself also ceased from his works as God did from His. Let us therefore be diligent to enter that rest, lest anyone fall according to the same example of disobedience. For the word of God is living and powerful, and sharper than any two-edged sword, piercing even to the division of soul and spirit, and of joints and marrow, and is a discerner of the thoughts and intents of the heart. And there is no creature hidden from His sight, but all things are naked and open to the eyes of Him to whom we must give account (Hebrews 4:1-12 NKJV).

To enter his rest we must be *obedient* to the voice of the Spirit despite whatever improbability, impossibility, challenge or force attempts to dissuade or intimidate us from following the Spirit's leading, specific instruction or clear direction from the Word.

DELIVERER

A **deliverer** is God's chosen instrument to establish righteousness and justice. The Lord sets his mantle of kingdom authority upon this individual to align all aspects of the supernatural work with his throne. The deliverer is charged to make visible God's celestial truths in the people and the structure.

Historically, biblical deliverers have been born into a hostile environment. Moses, Joseph, Elijah, and Jesus are a few examples of deliverers.

The deliverer learns to live in the constant dichotomy of favor and hostility and rise above it. The Lord anoints the deliverer as a catalyst of transformation in the earth.

Joseph, the eleventh son of Jacob, exemplifies how God molds a deliverer through environmental challenges and tribulation. The complete story of Joseph's life as God's chosen deliverer is recorded in Genesis 37-49. Joseph, although favored by his father Jacob, was despised by his brothers. He lived in a state of constant tension between the privilege of favor and the repercussions of hostility and jealousy. This is the lot of every deliverer.

The anointing on the deliverer is evident, as well as an aura of destiny. Their passion for justice and righteousness immediately distinguishes them from "players" who merely act the part, but in their hearts do not possess pure motives driven by a healthy fear of the Lord and his agape love.

Like Joseph, whose destiny was revealed in a dream, deliverers know they are destined for an assignment that will elevate them beyond what they are capable of doing in the natural. However, they possess a God-given confidence, which in Joseph's case, led him to share his dream of promotion with those who despised him. This untimely disclosure precipitated a series of events in Joseph's life that took him to the brink of utter destruction before the dream was prophetically fulfilled.

While God did not initiate those traumatic events—Joseph's betrayal by his brothers—being sold into slavery, taken to a foreign country and then cruelly sent to prison for a crime he did not commit, he used these tribulations to transform Joseph into his image. Without the tribulation, Joseph would not have learned how to persevere in adverse circumstances, work with people who were different from him in belief and culture, or how to be an effective administrator in a governmental system— the penal system of Egypt. Spiritually, he learned to stand alone, keep the faith, trust God despite the circumstances, and to hold on to the vision though his life had gone in the total opposite direction of his prophetic destiny.

Their innate sense of justice is the force behind the frustration and/or over-confidence of deliverers. This may cause them to move ahead of the timing of the Lord and attempt to enact their role in the flesh. Such was the case with Moses when he killed the Egyptian who was attacking the

Israelite slave (Exodus 2:11). Moses had a revelation of his deliverer destiny within him, but he moved into it in the flesh ahead of his anointing.

Moving out of the timing of the Lord resulted in Moses having to flee Egypt and spend the next forty years in the desert. This is another aspect of a deliverer; he or she will endure years of preparation for this role. God takes a deliverer through the "purging fire" to remove the dross from the individual's life. Malachi 3:3 (NLT) is descriptive of how the Lord refines us. *He will sit like a refiner of silver, burning away the **dross**. He will purify the Levites, refining them like gold and silver, so that they may once again offer acceptable sacrifices to the Lord* (emphasis added).

God prepares his servants through loving discipline. He reveals the dark places in our soul caused by a wound, offense or an iniquitous pattern passed down to us through our ancestors. These are areas of our spirit that have not been exposed to the light. Either we have willingly chosen the darkness, or we may be unaware the darkness exists. If we have refused to forgive an offense, that area of our soul is in darkness and not yielded to the Holy Spirit. Therefore, Satan "has something in us." In John 14:30 (KJV) Jesus, in his last encounter with the disciples before going to the cross assured his disciples that he would fulfill his role as deliverer of mankind from sin because Satan had no hold on him. There were no dark places in Jesus' soul that Satan could use to destroy him to prevent Jesus from fulfilling his role as our deliverer. *"Hereafter I will not talk much with you: for the prince of this world cometh, and hath nothing in me."*

I, Jan, have experienced the revelation of a dark place in my soul that had unknowingly hindered my moving into a new place in the Spirit. I had been seeking God in earnest, through study of the Word and prayer, for revelation of the hidden mysteries. I knew in my spirit God wanted to move me to a new place in him and to a greater anointing in ministry.

I traveled to the Upper Peninsula of Michigan to attend a retreat with my friend Sylvia. She, too, was hungry for the Lord and seeking to move into the deeper things of God. Prior to attending the retreat, I was staying with her at her apartment in the city of Marquette. One day I visited the local coffee shop. I was acquainted with one of the servers, Charlie, who was a master at the art of making the perfect cappuccino! Charlie and I had become acquainted on a previous visit a year and a half earlier. While he worked part-time at the coffee shop, he was actually an associate pastor in one of the local full-gospel churches. Charlie made my cappuccino and said he would sit down for a chat whenever a lull in customers allowed him the opportunity.

Soon Charlie strolled over to my table and sat down. He started the conversation by saying the last time I had seen him he and his wife had gone to a healing conference in California. He then told me, after traveling the great distance from Upper Michigan to Redding, California, the location of the healing conference, he was unable to receive the teaching and ministry in the sessions scheduled the first day.

Disturbed by his inability to spiritually engage, he sought the Lord as to what was wrong. He was greatly disappointed as he had come to the conference with great expectation to receive from the Lord an anointing for healing. That night, Charlie had a dream. He saw his parents deep in conversation. He heard one of his parents say: "We are not ready for this; we must do something about it."

When Charlie awoke in the morning he was greatly disturbed and perplexed in his spirit by the dream. He called his father and asked him if the conversation he had overheard in his dream was familiar. A dead silence followed. Finally, Charlie's Dad said, "Yes." His Dad then described the situation. Before Charlie was born his Mother became pregnant and his parents felt they were not ready to have children so they aborted the child.

Charlie was stunned. He explained that he could never understand why he had experienced so much *rejection*. In that moment, the Lord revealed to him that the spirit of rejection had been passed to him in the womb through the abortion of the first child. The curse of that iniquity came upon him. The transfer of an iniquitous pattern is scriptural. *The LORD is longsuffering, and of great mercy, forgiving **iniquity** and transgression, and by no means clearing the guilty, visiting the **iniquity** of the fathers upon the children unto the third and fourth generation* (Numbers 14:18 KJV, emphasis added).

Charlie said so much healing resulted because of that conversation. Since the time of the situation described in the dream, Charlie's parents had become believers; however, they had never divulged this sin to their son. What his parents had hid in the darkness was brought out into the light. As a result of bringing that dark area of their souls into the light, Charlie's parents and Charlie were set free. They experienced forgiveness and healing. Charlie's parents prayed and broke the iniquitous pattern of rejection off their family and future generations.

This story was the catalyst for my own dream that very night. In my dream, my husband, Bob, was on the phone with another woman. He was so engrossed in communicating with her that I became jealous of the manner in which he was speaking to her. I felt rejected and disregarded. I took the phone and told the woman in no uncertain terms, she was not to call or speak with my husband again. I awoke immediately. I knew this dream was from the Holy Spirit. I asked the Lord for the meaning of the dream. He responded, *"You must deal with the rejection."* I knew exactly what he meant based on the revelation of Charlie's dream.

That morning, Sylvia and I sat before the Lord praying and reading the Word. I recounted my conversation with Charlie and the dream I had the night before. She and I had both experienced much rejection in our respective childhood's and during our adult lives. After sharing Charlie's story, we had an immediate witness in our spirits. We repented before the Lord for allowing rejection to create in us a degenerate heart, which had hindered the work of the Holy Spirit in the areas of our lives where we had, or could, experience rejection. It had prevented the voice of God, or an inability to hear his voice, in this area of our lives.

We forgave our parents and broke the curse of rejection off our lives, our family members, and future generations. God led us in scripture to Ezekiel 16:1-16 (NKJV). He had given this passage of scripture to Sylvia years earlier tenderly revealing to her that it described her birth and life. It was for me too. We read the passage and wept.

Again the word of the LORD came to me, saying, "Son of man, cause Jerusalem to know her abominations and say, 'Thus says the Lord GOD to Jerusalem: "Your birth and your nativity are from the land of Canaan; your father was an Amorite and your mother a Hittite. As for your nativity, on the day you were born your navel cord was not cut, nor were you washed in water to cleanse you; you were not rubbed with salt nor wrapped in swaddling cloths. No eye pitied you, to do any of these things for you, to have compassion on you; but you were thrown out into the open field, when you yourself were loathed on the day you were born.

"And when I passed by you and saw you struggling in your own blood, I said to you in your blood, 'Live!' Yes, I said to you in your blood, 'Live!' I made you thrive like a plant in the field; and you grew, matured, and became very beautiful. Your breasts were formed, your hair grew, but you

were naked and bare. "When I passed by you again and looked upon you, indeed your time was the time of love; so I spread My wing over you and covered your nakedness. Yes, I swore an oath to you and entered into a covenant with you, and you became Mine," says the Lord GOD.

"Then I washed you in water; yes, I thoroughly washed off your blood, and I anointed you with oil. I clothed you in embroidered cloth and gave you sandals of badger skin; I clothed you with fine linen and covered you with silk. I adorned you with ornaments, put bracelets on your wrists, and a chain on your neck. And I put a jewel in your nose, earrings in your ears, and a beautiful crown on your head. Thus you were adorned with gold and silver, and your clothing was of fine linen, silk, and embroidered cloth. You ate pastry of fine flour, honey, and oil. You were exceedingly beautiful, and succeeded to royalty. Your fame went out among the nations because of your beauty, for it was perfect through My splendor which I had bestowed on you," says the Lord GOD.

"But you trusted in your own beauty, played the harlot because of your fame, and poured out your harlotry on everyone passing by who would have it. You took some of your garments and adorned multicolored high places for yourself, and played the harlot on them. Such things should not happen, nor be.

Then we repented of our own iniquities. We had asked the Lord to cleanse us with hyssop like David to make us whiter than snow. Moreover, we sought the Lord to cleanse us through the washing of the Word. He led us to Deuteronomy 23:5 (NKJV), *Nevertheless the LORD your God would not listen to Balaam, but the LORD your God turned the curse into a blessing for you, because the LORD your God loves you.* Through this scripture, God showed us that he had turned the curse into a blessing. Now that we were cleansed and the curse broken, Proverbs 26:2 was operational—a causeless curse could not come.

We looked up *iniquity*[1] in Webster's New World Dictionary. It is defined as "lack of righteousness or justice; wickedness or unrighteous act." Iniquity is generational in nature; it reflects a pattern or a bent toward certain sins that originated in your ancestral line and have been passed down to you through your parents. For example, addictions are the result of an iniquitous generational pattern to self-medicate. If investigated, an alcoholic, drug addict, or some other form of addict, will have this same pattern evident in other family members, or members of a prior generation. The Bible clearly states an iniquitous pattern is passed down through generations. *The LORD is longsuffering and abundant in mercy, forgiving iniquity and transgression; but He by no means clears the guilty, visiting the iniquity of the fathers on the children to the third and fourth generation* (Numbers 14:18 KJV).

Rejection [2] is defined as "to deny acceptance, care, love, etc. to someone." We were sealed. There was no open door for Satan. We received a rhema word from the Lord, "*I will have a bride without spot or wrinkle. I will have a clean bride.*" We then read Deuteronomy 28:1-14 and decreed the blessings of obedience over our lives.

If God has called you to be a deliverer, he will first deliver you from "yourself"—your bondages and dark places in your soul. Satan cannot have "anything" in you if you are to be a chosen vessel of a supernatural work.

FORERUNNER

A **forerunner** is an individual who has received God's vision. He or she is obedient to the voice of the Lord, following the leadings of the Holy Spirit. A forerunner breaks through into new territory in the spirit with God, and then sets a course for others to follow. The apostle Paul experienced a number of revelations and heavenly visitations that prepared him to breakthrough both spiritually and in the natural, to expand the gospel into new territory, that of the gentiles—2 Cor.12:1-7.

A forerunner restores lost truths and unveils "truths" to the body. God chose Paul, a former Pharisee and scholar of the Old Testament Scriptures, to unveil the truth to the church that they had been chosen to be in the Messiah before the foundation of the world—Eph. 1:4. In our present church age, the Bible is complete and the unveiled truths are a deeper, revelatory understanding of the text.

The majority of the body of Christ has *lost* the true meaning of repentance in salvation. Therefore, people make confessions based on emotion and a little prayer, not true *repentance*. In a forerunner capacity, author and prophetic teacher, John Bevere, has been instrumental in restoring the truth of true repentance to the church.[3]

The Leader: Deliverer And Forerunner

A forerunner is the instrument through which God reveals the pattern of the supernatural work and the blueprints for building it. The Lord imparts a breaker anointing upon a forerunner. This anointing breaks demonic opposition to restore what was lost and brings to Earth the new thing that God is doing. It operates through individuals as they are intimately connected to God in prayer—repentance, petition, intercession, supplication, declaration, etc; they come before the Lord as a cleansed, surrendered vessel willing to wrestle in prayer for God to breakthrough before them as the Lord did for David when he went out to fight the Philistines at Baal Perazim (2 Samuel 5:17-25).

While both functions, *deliverer* and *forerunner*, must be operative in the individual, one may be more dominant. Moses functioned foremost as a deliverer; however, the Lord brought Joshua along side of Moses as a forerunner. Moses delegated a portion of his mantle, along with the authority to carry it out, to Joshua. Moses did this publicly before all of Israel, so that there would be no doubt as to the scope of Joshua's authority and accountability.

Then Moses said to the Lord, "O Lord, you are the God who gives breath to all creatures. Please appoint a new man as leader for the community. Give them someone who will guide them wherever they go and will lead them into battle, so the community of the Lord will not be like sheep without a shepherd."

The Lord replied, "Take Joshua son of Nun, who has the Spirit in him, and lay your hands on him. Present him to Eleazar the priest before the whole community, and publicly commission him to lead the people. Transfer some of your authority to him so the whole community of Israel will obey him. When direction from the Lord is needed, Joshua will stand before Eleazar the priest, who will use the Urim—one of the sacred lots cast before the Lord—to determine his will. This is how Joshua and the rest of the community of Israel will determine everything they should do" (Numbers 27:15-21 NLT).

Moses had led the Israelites out of their Egyptian bondage and then spent the next forty years guiding the people as God dealt with their spiritual bondages. During this period, God gave Moses the Ten

Commandments and the pattern and blueprint of the tabernacle. The law was God's pattern for righteousness and justice or the Government of God. The tabernacle was God's blueprint for worship.

Joshua was present on the mountain with Moses. But he was not taken up into the cloud of God's presence to receive the law and the blueprint of the tabernacle. *So Moses arose with his assistant Joshua, and Moses went up to the mountain of God* (Exodus 24:13 NKJV). In this instance, Moses functioned in the forerunner role receiving the blueprint of the law and tabernacle. However, Joshua learned how to function as a forerunner by shadowing Moses. Consequently, when Moses sent twelve leaders to spy out the Promised Land *to provide a blueprint of it and its inhabitants*—Joshua was among the chosen (See Numbers 13 and 14).

After 40 days, the twelve spies returned with their report. Ten spies reported the land was indeed fertile as God had promised—a land of milk and honey. Despite its natural abundance, they did not believe it could be conquered, as the inhabitants were warriors of superior physical and military strength. Caleb and Joshua countered the negative report with words of faith and life, giving them favor in God's eyes.

> *But Joshua the son of Nun and Caleb the son of Jephunneh, who were among those who had spied out the land, tore their clothes; and they spoke to all the congregation of the children of Israel, saying: "The land we passed through to spy out is an exceedingly good land. If the LORD delights in us, then He will bring us into this land and give it to us, 'a land which flows with milk and honey.' Only do not rebel against the LORD, nor fear the people of the land, for they are our bread; their protection has departed from them, and the LORD is with us. Do not fear them* (Numbers 14:6-9 NKJV).

God's hand was behind the decision to send Joshua to spy out the Promised Land. The Lord had chosen Joshua as his vessel to conquer the land; therefore, he must have the blueprint. Because Moses had mentored Joshua, allowing him to be present at critical junctures as God worked through him in the roles of deliverer and forerunner, Joshua's faith in God, not Moses, was stable. When faced with overwhelming opposition, his faith was not shaken. Spying out the land was a way God tested Joshua for his forerunner role. Throughout his life, Joshua would function foremost as a forerunner.

When Moses received the initial vision of the Promised Land, Joshua was at his side. He sought the Lord with Moses and spent time in the Lord's presence. Although neither Moses nor Joshua was aware of it at the time, a significant portion of the vision would be fulfilled through Joshua. Joshua's role required he be both a spiritual and physical warrior. As he sat before the Lord, he became a strong spiritual warrior such that when confronted with the warriors of flesh in the Promised Land, they did not intimidate him.

Whenever Moses went out to the Tent of Meeting, all the people would get up and stand in the entrances of their own tents. They would all watch Moses until he disappeared inside. As he went into the tent, the pillar of cloud would come down and hover at its entrance while the Lord spoke with Moses. When the people saw the cloud standing at the entrance of the tent, they would stand and bow down in front of their own tents. Inside the Tent of Meeting, the Lord would speak to Moses face to face, as one speaks to a friend. Afterward Moses would return to the camp, but the young man who assisted him, Joshua son of Nun, would remain behind in the Tent of Meeting (Exodus 33:8-11 NLT).

What distinguishes leadership in a supernatural work from a mere program is the forerunner function. The forerunner receives a divine blueprint. He or she does not implement a replica of something given to a different part of the body of Christ. This is where *transformation* is released as the work is infused with *resurrection power*. The forerunner is not relying on skills and abilities; rather the individual is surrendered to the Holy Spirit—having received a mantle for the mission and an anointing to carry it out.

The anointing of a forerunner is a *breaker anointing*. A breaker anointing overcomes demonic opposition through God pulling down strongholds of the enemy in the spiritual realm, prior to physically taking the territory. *For though we walk in the flesh, we do not war according to the flesh. For the weapons of our warfare are not carnal but mighty in God for pulling down strongholds, casting down arguments and every high thing that exalts itself against the knowledge of God, bringing every thought into captivity to the obedience of Christ* (2 Corinthians 10:3-5 KJV).

This spiritual demolition prior to the physical work is critical; it is the element most often overlooked that may later be the ruin of a strategic effort. Joshua did not neglect to sit in the Lord's presence to receive divine revelation and to engage in spiritual warfare.

As Joshua was sizing up the city of Jericho prior to receiving the divine battle plan, God opened up the spiritual realm and Joshua saw what appeared to be a man with a drawn sword.

When Joshua was near the town of Jericho, he looked up and saw a man standing in front of him with sword in hand. Joshua went up to him and demanded, "Are you friend or foe?" "Neither one," he replied. "I am the commander of the Lord's army." At this, Joshua fell with his face to the ground in reverence. "I am at your command," Joshua said. "What do you want your servant to do?" The commander of the Lord's army replied, "Take off your sandals, for the place where you are standing is holy." And Joshua did as he was told (Joshua 5:13-15 NLT).

Joshua realized the battle was going to be fought in the spiritual realm first. The heavenly host would engage the demonic forces to the pulling down of the stronghold before the physical wall of Jericho would fall, and the enemy in the natural could be conquered. Joshua surrendered to the Spirit and followed his orders exactly.

Like Joshua, forerunners break through into new territory with the Lord. They blaze a trail in the spirit that others can then follow. It was as forerunners, that our prayer group leadership broke through the demonic opposition of Leviathan. God gave us the pattern of the vow. God revealed a breakthrough pattern in dealing with Leviathan that others can use to displace the Leviathan spirit.

At the inception of the "church" in the first century, the believers walked in resurrection power such that people touched by the Apostle Peter's shadow were healed. *As a result of the apostles' work, sick people were brought out into the streets on beds and mats so that Peter's shadow might fall across some of them as he went by* (Acts 5:15 NLT).

Slowly, over time, the power and the truths the first century church walked in were lost to the body of Christ. God has been restoring those truths and his power ever since. Martin Luther's disgust regarding the Catholic Church selling indulgences—basically a *"get out of jail"* card from Purgatory—prompted him to seek the scriptures for the truth. The scriptures revealed "the just shall walk by faith." *For therein is the righteousness of God revealed from faith to faith: as it is written, the just shall live by faith* (Romans 1:17 KJV). God used Martin Luther as a forerunner to restore this truth to the body of Christ.

Forerunners must be willing to endure persecution, ridicule and rejection. The process of restoration of power and truth to the body of Christ means a stronghold of the enemy must be unseated. A forerunner must be equipped for spiritual battle, and recognize that people are not the enemy, they are merely captive to the positions the enemy has enticed them to hold. For example, *cessationists* believe that the "power gifts" prophecy, healing, speaking in tongues and casting out demons ceased after the apostles laid the foundation of the church. These gifts were needed to lay the foundation, but subsequently, have ceased and are no longer available to the body of Christ.

Consequently, the restoration of faith healing ministries in the body of Christ has met fierce opposition. Oral Roberts and Kenneth Hagin were forerunners in faith healing. As such, they endured much persecution from cessationists in the body who believed their beliefs were heretical and the healings demonic.

If God is calling us as a chosen vessel to lead a supernatural work, we must stop and count the cost. God does not want over-zealous vessels operating through their own skills and abilities and calling it the "anointing." He is seeking vessels willing to undergo purging and cleansing; those who allow him to mold them through persecution, hardship and trials. Upon those "emptied of themselves and of no reputation" he places his mantle and anointing. These vessels, fashioned by the Potter's hand, are formed into deliverers and forerunners.

Chapter 8

FASHIONED BY THE POTTER

To be molded into his image means we must be spun on the Potter's wheel. As in the natural, spinning on the supernatural Potter's wheel is a somewhat dizzying and confusing experience! We aren't quite sure what God is doing—stuff is flying in all directions; it hurts and all we want to do is get off. If we can hold fast during this fashioning, we will become a "solid" pot without cracks; and few, if any flaws—a vessel of honor that the Lord can use.

What is God doing when he is molding us on the Potter's wheel for a supernatural work? He is fashioning in us the criteria of a governing leader in his kingdom, with the objective of placing the mantle of our mission upon us. He will then bring others into our sphere of influence to co-labor with us. According to God's governmental structure, a governing leader is an *elder*; those that support and co-labor with the elders are *deacons* (see *Supernatural Work Structure* in Chapter 6). For the purpose of simplification, we will identify elders as governing leaders and deacons as support or co-laboring leaders.

CRITERIA OF A GOVERNING LEADER

When God calls us to lead a supernatural work, he will place his government upon us as is described in Isaiah 9:6-7 (NKJV).

For unto us a Child is born, unto us a Son is given; And the government will be upon His shoulder. And His name will be called Wonderful, Counselor, Mighty God, Everlasting Father, Prince of Peace. Of the increase of His government and peace there will be no end, upon the throne of David and over His kingdom, to order it and establish it with judgment and justice from that time forward, even forever. The zeal of the Lord of hosts will perform this.

God's government is based on righteousness and justice. The function of a governing leader is a serious matter to God. A governmental leader will undergo rigorous, long-term preparation. A Moses, David or Paul is formed through purging and through fire. God selectively chooses those he wants to raise up in kingdom governance. It is our role to recognize and cooperate with God's choice.

God is foremost concerned with our heart — which forms our character. As our character is molded by God, our heart motivations align with his throne — righteousness and justice, and these foundations shape our character. I (Jan), was first introduced to the first four characteristics in a study Bible; however, an overarching characteristic was missing, *submission*. These five characteristics are common to all governmental leaders : 1) hiddenness; 2) brokenness; 3) humility; 4) solitude; and 5) submission.

Hiddenness. Individuals chosen for governmental leadership will experience seasons and years of obscurity. For example, Moses spent 40 years on the backside of the desert herding sheep. All the while, God was forming in him the character attributes, including patience, to lead an entire nation out of captivity! God had placed in Moses' heart his destiny to free his people. Initially, Moses attempted to do it in his own strength by killing the Egyptian, thinking the Israelites would know and understand his purpose. They did not because it was not God's timing. Moses had not yet been forged into the vessel that could carry the level of governmental kingdom authority required to set the people free. We must allow God to do the work needed in these individuals before releasing them to their destiny. Moses released himself before his time and suffered greatly for it.

Brokenness. Before God can exalt an individual for a governing role, that person must be broken of self-will, ambition, pride, and confidence in their own abilities. David was declared by God as a *"man after mine own heart,"* (Acts 13:22 KJV). God could say this about David because he had been "broken" repeatedly. Although he had been anointed for kingship as a teenager, he spent years as a fugitive running from King Saul whom he had served faithfully. A broken person understands the cost of forgiveness. He or she has experienced injustice, injury and persecution without falling prey to a root of bitterness. The Psalms provide a record of David's brokenness before God. It was David who penned *"a broken and contrite heart O God, thou wilt not despise,"* (Psalm 51:17 KJV).

Humility. Humility is difficult to define but easily recognizable. It is the result of a heart that has experienced true repentance and brokenness. It is the fruit of a life that has faced adversity and overcome obstacles, and prevailed in the face of insurmountable odds. One that understands who he or she is in Christ, but does not seek to exalt him or herself based upon that knowledge. Rather, the recognition of being a holy priesthood and co-heir with Christ is the impetus to serve the body not lord over it. When the Lord decreed David's house would be established forever, it was the spirit of humility in King David that questioned *"Who am I, O Lord God, and what is my family, that you have given me all this?"* (1 Chron. 17:16 NLT).

Solitude. Without prolonged periods of solitude, God cannot develop our character or reveal his plan and purposes to our hearts. It was during a season of concentrated solitude, including a stint in the deserts of Arabia, that Paul received his manifold revelations of Christ including being taken into the third heaven and seeing things he had no human words to describe (2 Cor. 12:2-4; Gal. 1:11-17). Jesus retreated to deserted places alone to commune with the Father and to receive his assignments. In these periods of solitude, Jesus engaged in intense spiritual warfare and received strengthening from angels.

Submission. Without full heart submission to God's authority and his delegated authority over us, we can embody all the other characteristics but when faced with testing, calamity, adversity, or opposition we will falter as a deliverer/forerunner and default to an independent spirit. We will go our own way, departing from our position and assignment, becoming a law unto ourselves. Jesus evidenced total heart submission in the garden of Gethsemane as he struggled to submit his will to the Father's.

Clearly, these criteria demonstrate the calling of a governing leader in a supernatural work is a *process* of purging, cleansing and character development. They form a line of demarcation separating those who are merely *interested* from the truly *committed*. God's purpose is to mold us into his image, so that we show that image to the world. It is his image in us that attracts the world and resources (i.e., finances, materials, favor to gain a position of influence) to his throne. As we lead with righteousness and justice, his kingdom government is established in the earth.

MANTLES

When God calls you to a supernatural work he places a mantle upon you. *A mantle is a measure of authority, stature, and God-given ability including spiritual gifts, to fulfill the mission of your calling.* The mantle he places upon you will be recognized by others. Those designated to be a part of the work will be attracted to you, and submit to the governmental anointing of your mantle.

The anointing on your life will flow through your mantle. Your mantle functions in the same manner as a cell phone. God transmits the anointing (radio waves) to your vessel which flows through your mantle (cell phone). This results in the power of God manifesting to transmit his divine purpose in each situation. For example, if God has called you to a supernatural work in the area of healing, an anointing for healing will flow through your mantle of ministry in healing.

A mantle is received through God's grace. We cannot earn it and most do not choose it. However, we can aspire to a mantle God has placed on someone else in an area he is calling us as well. For example, God chose Elisha as Elijah's successor to the office of prophet to Israel. Elisha aspired to the mantle that rested on Elijah, and he asked to build upon that mantle, with a double portion of it.

God chooses you for a supernatural work and he places a mantle upon you to accomplish it. It is a work of the Spirit in and upon you, in which the flow of the seven-fold Holy Spirit (Isaiah 11:2) energizes and strengthens your spirit with wisdom and understanding, counsel and might, knowledge and the fear of the Lord in the mission he has called you to fulfill.

WALKING IN THE MANTLE

Moses received his anointing and mantle after being formed in the criteria of a governing leader for 40 years in the desert. When he received the mantle to lead the children of Israel out of bondage, God created the setting for him to flow in his anointing. He gave him supernatural ability to do signs and wonders. He prepares us for the work he has called us to perform.

As we cannot accomplish a supernatural work alone, God brings others to govern with us. The Lord brought Aaron, Miriam and Joshua to work alongside Moses and support his mantle. The proverbial "no man is an island" is true of a supernatural work. God appoints others to co-labor with us in the area of governing and accomplishing the work. Our part is to seek God for his choices and then to commission those leaders. The first requirement in seeking co-laboring leaders is heart motivation.

Heart Motivation

A supernatural work requires that a leader is able to both pioneer and nurture. A Godly leader's biblical mandate is to *influence* people. The objective is to motivate others to grow in holiness and reach their kingdom potential. To accomplish this monumental task, Godly leaders are concerned with character, motive and agenda.

Without a divine objective to work toward, and a positive move toward holiness of character, motivation can become a manipulative tool to be used as a "means to an end." In his seminal book on biblical, servant leadership, Don Howell, Jr. emphasizes a crucial point from scripture. "*…God is about the business of extending his lordship over the "hearts" of people who have responded in repentance and faith to his offer of forgiveness (Mt. 4:17, 19)*".[1] **Motivation is a heart matter.** With this in view, how we deal with the hearts of his people is a very serious matter.

To motivate from the right heart perspective, our purpose must align with a divine blueprint. As Howell defines in *Servants of the Servant: A*

Biblical Theology of Leadership, this blueprint presumes that leadership in a supernatural work:

- is people-oriented rather than solely program-driven
- focuses on the spiritual maturity of individuals and the community
- is kingdom-oriented over organization-driven—it seeks to motivate and support people to reach their kingdom potential[2].

Co-laboring leaders of a supernatural work are chosen through a divine "call," no less significant than that of Moses, Samuel, Peter, or Paul. However, how you *enact* leadership is a matter of your own heart initiative for which you are accountable to God. He has entrusted to you the nurture and care of his children.

Seeking and Commissioning Leaders

Biblically, how do we seek and commission leaders? Moses was chosen for leadership through a divine call (Exodus 3:1-14). He was privileged to commune with God face-to-face. When the Lord decreed Moses would not enter the Promised Land because of his disobedience in striking the rock, Moses accepted his fate and began to pray for a man with a shepherd's heart to replace him. God chose Joshua; however, in this delegated leadership role, Joshua was required to seek divine guidance through the Aaronic priesthood rather than face-to-face guidance of the Lord.

> *Who shall go out and come in before them, leading them out and bringing them in, that the congregation of the Lord may not be as sheep which have no shepherd. The Lord said to Moses, Take Joshua son of Nun, a man in whom is the Spirit, and lay your hand upon him; and set him before Eleazar the priest and all the congregation and give him a charge in their sight. And put some of your honor and authority upon him, that all the congregation of the Israelites may obey him." He shall stand before Eleazar the priest, who shall inquire for him before the Lord by the judgment of the Urim (one of two articles in the priest's breastplate worn when asking counsel of the Lord for the people). At Joshua's word the people shall go out and come in, both he and all the Israelite congregation with him (Numbers 27:17-20 AMP).*

Similarly, Samuel was directed by the Lord to the family of Jesse in Bethlehem to choose the next king. While Samuel, in the natural, would have chosen Jesse's first-born son Eliab, due to his stature and appearance, God rejected him. The Lord told Samuel his primary criterion is not appearance, resumé, or skills—*it is the heart* (I Samuel 16:1-13).

In the New Testament, Peter was chosen as a stone to lay the foundation of the church upon Christ—the Rock. This is surprising considering Peter's character initially was erratic, unreliable, overconfident, affectionate, impulsive, fervent, bold, rash, well-meaning, and eager. In other words, Peter was a bundle of conflicting thoughts and emotions.[3]

Individuals God has chosen for leadership may be quite raw and unrefined; nevertheless, each will possess a heart that chases after God. Such an individual is malleable because he or she can be guided and corrected by the Holy Spirit. They have a heart that is submitted to the Divine will and can come under authority.

SEEKING PROCESS

According to scripture, the first step in seeking leaders is *prayer*. It requires the guidance of the Holy Spirit as to God's choice. We see the outward appearance but only he sees the heart. Secondly, scripture defines the characteristics of those that have leadership potential.

In the eighteenth chapter of Exodus, Moses' father-in-law Jethro, visited the camp of the Israelites and observed Moses judging the people from dawn to dusk every day. Moses tried to handle all the issues himself. Wisely, Jethro suggested to Moses that he delegate the responsibility of leadership to those most capable in character and ability.

The next day, Moses took his seat to hear the people's disputes against each other. They waited before him from morning till evening.

When Moses' father-in-law saw all that Moses was doing for the people, he asked, "What are you really accomplishing here? Why are you trying to do all this alone while everyone stands around you from morning till evening?"

Moses replied, "Because the people come to me to get a ruling from God. When a dispute arises, they come to me, and I am the one who settles the case between the quarreling parties. I inform the people of God's decrees and give them his instructions."

"This is not good!" Moses' father-in-law exclaimed. "You're going to wear yourself out—and the people, too. This job is too heavy a burden for you to handle all by yourself. Now listen to me, and let me give you a word of advice, and may God be with you. You should continue to be the people's representative before God, bringing their disputes to him. Teach them God's decrees, and give them his instructions. Show them how to conduct their lives. But select from all the people some capable, honest men who fear God and hate bribes. Appoint them as leaders over groups of one thousand, one hundred, fifty, and ten. They should always be available to solve the people's common disputes, but have them bring the major cases to you. Let the leaders decide the smaller matters themselves. They will help you carry the load, making the task easier for you. If you follow this advice, and if God commands you to do so, then you will be able to endure the pressures, and all these people will go home in peace."

Moses listened to his father-in-law's advice and followed his suggestions. He chose capable men from all over Israel and appointed them as leaders over the people. He put them in charge of groups of one thousand, one hundred, fifty, and ten. These men were always available to solve the people's common disputes. They brought the major cases to Moses, but they took care of the smaller matters themselves (Exodus 18:13-27 NLT).

Jethro identified five characteristics to seek in choosing leaders to support a supernatural work: 1) able individuals; 2) fear God; 3) possess integrity; 4) not covetous; and 5) span of influence.

Able Individuals

In the King James Version of the Bible, Moses is instructed to seek out "able" (capable) individuals. The Hebrew word for "able" is *chayil*[4] which means virtuous, worthy, strong, valor, train, a force, substance and war. Therefore, capable individuals have the potential to accomplish the task. They are chosen for their inherent potential, not for political "usefulness" or charismatic appeal. *Ability* in this sense means the capability—mentally, spiritually and physically to fulfill the assignment. It does not mean they are in complete possession of all the attributes at the onset.

Capable individuals possess a *teachable* spirit. They can be trained and are willing to be mentored and submit to authority. They are willing to accept instruction, guidance and correction. They seek divine wisdom and operate with discernment and discretion. Most importantly, they operate offensively—as a spiritual force, willing and trained spiritual warriors.

Fear God

Those chosen for support leadership roles are not *"people pleasers."* They guide, instruct and correct according to scripture, not cultural considerations or political correctness. These individuals are rightly prioritized. They maintain an intimate relationship with God first, with ministry and job responsibilities flowing out of that relationship.

They are morally upright—*they walk the talk*. They speak the truth and are trustworthy. They do *not* play "favorites" or foster a "good old' boys" club of *you take care of me and I'll take care of you* mentality that allows for bribes, favoritism and nepotism. Most importantly, they are filled with the Holy Spirit and focus on being spirit-led over task driven (see Acts 6:1-7 regarding overseers).

Possess Integrity

Support leaders are committed. They can be counted on to do what they say they will do and accomplish the work on schedule. They speak truth through God's heart—with mercy and compassion. They accurately assess people and situations by discerning God's heart; then take appropriate steps to resolve problems, issues and contentions. They focus on relationship—showing honor and respect for the individual although they may disagree with the person's reasoning or position.

The formation of Godly character is a hallmark of these individuals. As Titus 1:5-9 and 1 Timothy 3:1-7 advise, those chosen in a leadership capacity should possess (or are actively working toward) a stable, balanced temperament. They are self-controlled in that they demonstrate sensible caution. They exhibit wholesome attitudes and winsome behaviors — not coarse or crude, rather they command the respect of others.

Those chosen for leadership should not be overly aggressive, but peaceable exhibiting gentleness in dealing with difficult people and situations. Co-laboring leaders should actively pursue a life-style of holiness devoted to purity in thought and behaviors. They ought to be a lover of that which is good; a person who cultivates the qualities (love, justice, righteousness, etc.) that reflect the attributes of God. Such individuals practice self-management to the degree they are disciplined and moderate in exercise, appetite and sexual desires.

Not Covetous

Individuals chosen for co-laboring leadership must be free of the love of money. In other words, everything does not revolve around the "bottom line." They are co-laboring because of a call and a conviction that they are accomplishing a supernatural work ordained of God. They are seeking "eternal" rewards over present remuneration or recognition. These individuals will not be ambitiously jockeying for position or favor. Consequently, in most situations, it is ill-advised to place recent converts into a support leadership position. Recent converts need sufficient time to develop a relationship with the Lord and experience some humbling experiences that temper one's self-confidence (see I Timothy 3:1-7). The spirit of pride can arise in the heart of a person exalted too soon, and may result in a great fall for the individual and damage to the supernatural work.

Span of Influence

Those chosen in co-laboring leadership should demonstrate the ability to manage their current span of influence. Therefore, with the delegation of responsibility, the oversight leadership must release the authority to the individual to handle everything within their sphere of accountability. As they grow in skill and ability to manage greater responsibility, their span of influence should increase.

The Bible outlines for co-laboring positions, we are to seek individuals who possess (are actively pursuing) the above characteristics. In essence, we are to seek leaders with the proper heart motivation, evidence of character, and submission to God's agenda—no hidden agendas.[5] As surmised from the above criteria, leadership in a supernatural work is contingent upon wholesome moral character.

COMMISSIONING PROCESS

It is interesting to note that individuals in the Bible were not just handed a task or thrust into a leadership role. Leaders were identified and commissioned before the assembly *prior* to taking on the mantle of leadership. In Numbers 27:18-20, Joshua stood before the high priest and the entire congregation for his commissioning as Moses' successor. In Acts 6:6, the apostles laid hands on the individuals before the assembly. The apostolic leaders prayed over them, and gave them the authority to carry out their role before any training or instruction! This indicates there was a formal commissioning process that identified these individuals as leaders before the people and a formal designation of authority. The Numbers passage clearly indicates this was done to give the person honor before the people, so the congregation understood the individual's word carried weight and was to be obeyed.

JESUS' MINISTRY MODEL

Not only is the seeking and commissioning process important, but how a leader *enacts* the role of leadership will have a significant impact on fulfilling the purposes of God in implementing the vision and goals of the supernatural work. We are all aware of the casualties in leadership—those burned-out or led astray into immorality or love of the world. Jesus is our role model for enacting leadership that will result in staying the course and finishing the race.

Engagement and Withdrawal

As author Don Howell illustrates in *Servants of the Servant: A Biblical Theology of Leadership*, Jesus' pattern for ministry combined times of active, engaged ministry with periods of withdrawal for prayer, guidance and spiritual and physical restoration.[6] Jesus engaged in periods of intense activity of preaching and body ministry. Mark 6:6b (NLT) records, *Then Jesus went from village to village, teaching the people.* However, he purposely sought times of withdrawal from the incessant demands of the crowd. Further in chapter 6, Jesus instructed his disciples to get into a boat leaving the crowds on the shore while he went alone up into the hills to pray (6:46).

Often when we are involved in a supernatural work, we may become overwhelmed by the enormity of the task. However, we must always keep Christ as the example we follow. Jesus understood that to do the work of ministry, he could not rely on his own strength or be driven by the vast need surrounding him. Rather, Jesus depended solely on the empowering and filling of the Holy Spirit, and then did only those things assigned to him by the Father (what he saw the Father doing, John 5:19-20).

If we are to fulfill the demands of a supernatural work, we must follow the pattern Jesus modeled for us of active ministry and periods of withdrawal. We learn to rest despite the stresses placed upon us because of the work and the expectations of others.

MISSION

The Lord releases mantles over the founding leaders of the work. This mantle remains on the leader for the duration of the mission. The mission is the specific supernatural work for which God has revealed the blueprint and called us to accomplish in the earth. When the leader departs (God removes him from the work) the mantle stays with the mission. The leader publicly transfers the mantle to the successor(s), as illustrated by Moses when he transferred the mantle of leadership to Joshua. Similarly, Elijah transferred the prophet's mantle to Elisha, his successor, who operated in a double-portion of the anointing of that mantle. This was evidenced in twice the miracles being performed through the anointing of the mantle on Elisha.

The mission is greater than one individual. The Bible supplies numerous examples of God initiating the mission through one individual, but never implementing or completing it through just one person. For instance, Moses was chosen to initiate the exodus from Egypt; however, it was Joshua who achieved the conquest of the Promised Land. Abraham was chosen as the Father of the nation of Israel, but it was his great-grandson Jacob who fathered the twelve sons that populated twelve tribes that formed the nation.

The mission of a supernatural work is a joint effort of the power of God and human instruments as pliable vessels in the Potter's hand. The Potter will shape the vessels in such manner that they can only accomplish this great work by the power of his Spirit.

GOVERNING STRUCTURE

As the graphic below depicts, a supernatural governing structure is centered on the cross and submitted to it. This framework is non-hierarchical in positioning, with all leadership under the mantle and anointing of the governing leader. To operate effectively, everyone must function in unity with the Spirit, internalizing the vision so that the governing and support leaders are working as a unified force to accomplish the mission.

Once the governing leader has fulfilled his/her part of the mission, the mantle will typically pass to one of the co-laboring leaders who has functioned under the mantle and anointing of the governing leader. For example, Joshua operated under the mantle and anointing of Moses before assuming the governing leadership role.

GOVERNING STRUCTURE

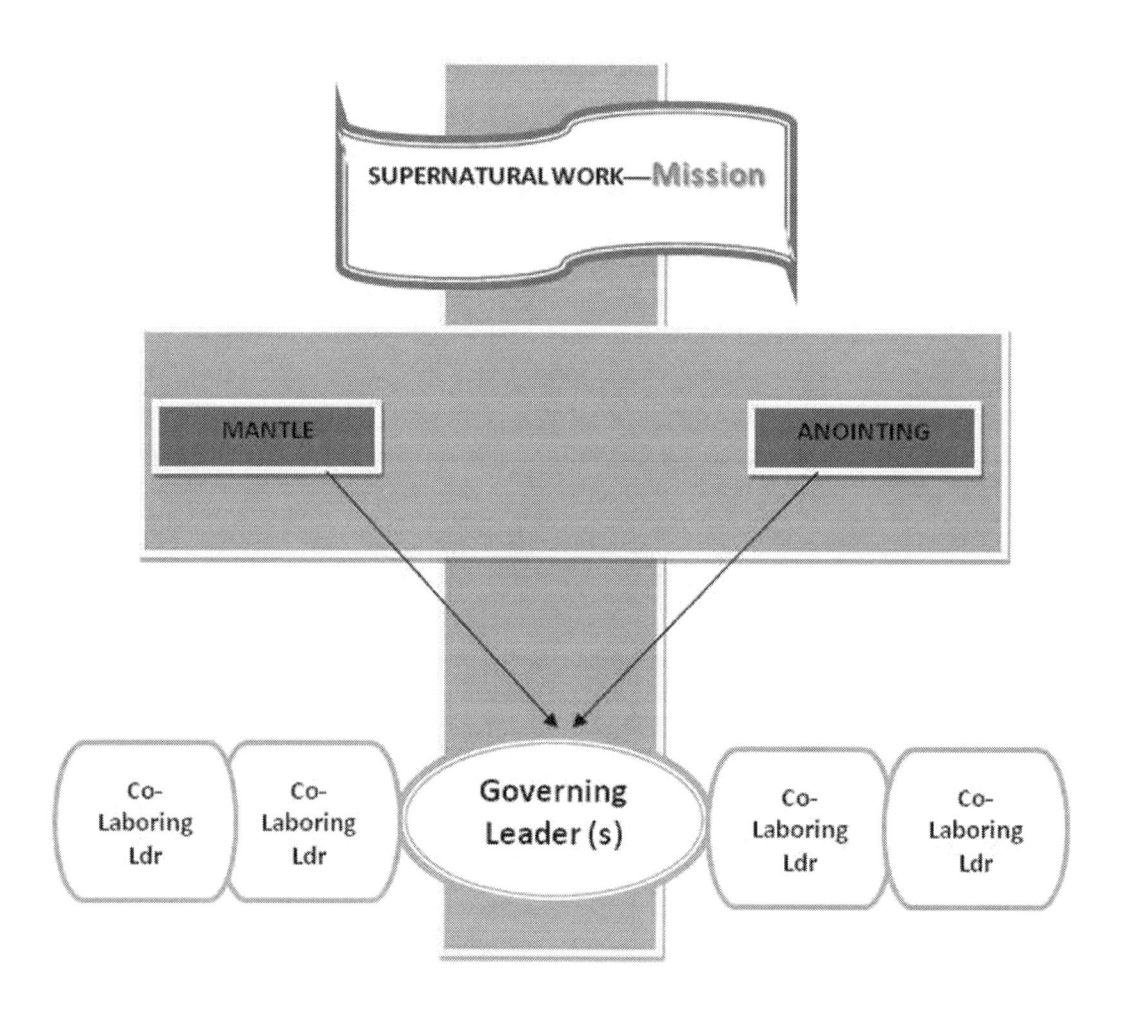

SUPERNATURAL WORK—Mission

MANTLE

ANOINTING

Co-Laboring Ldr | Co-Laboring Ldr | Governing Leader(s) | Co-Laboring Ldr | Co-Laboring Ldr

Chapter 9

BUILDING WITH GOD'S HEART

God's primary concern is people. As outlined in Chapter 7, a forerunner and deliverer lay the groundwork of a supernatural work. In any supernatural work, whether it is birthing "a new thing" on a foundation laid by a new forerunner/deliverer, or "a new thing" on the foundation of a *previous* forerunner/deliverer, the people are integral to, and intimately a part of, the building process.

When God has revealed his pattern and released his plans into your spirit, and you have laid the spiritual foundation of the house (supernatural work), it is time to build.

Building is a process. The Lord prophetically spoke through Isaiah, how the Messiah was to deliver and build the house of Israel into the Kingdom.

> *I, the Lord, have called you to demonstrate my righteousness. I will take you by the hand and guard you, and I will give you to my people, Israel, as a symbol of my covenant with them. And you will be a*

light to guide the nations. You will open the eyes of the blind. You will free the captives from prison, releasing those who sit in dark dungeons (Isaiah 42:6-7 NLT).

Jesus is our model of a master builder. The above passage outlines the ways and means we are to build with people.

Light to Guide Nations

We are instructed to be a *light*. In Matthew 5:14 (NKJV) Jesus declares, *"You are the light of the world. A city set on a hill that cannot be hidden."* As master builders working with co-laborers, everything must be done in the light. Jesus functioned in this manner. At Jesus' inquisition by the high priest before his crucifixion, he was questioned concerning his doctrine and his disciples,

> *Jesus answered him, "I spoke openly to the world. I always taught in synagogues and in the temple, where the Jews always meet, and in secret I have said nothing. Why do you ask Me? Ask those who have heard Me what I said to them. Indeed they know what I said." (John 18:20-21 NKJV).*

Jesus was "open" with those who co-labored with him. He conducted his ministry in such a manner that there were no "hidden agendas." He taught openly in the temple in the presence of the Sadducees and Pharisees, who vigorously opposed his teaching. He did not keep "secrets" from those who labored with him, or from those that opposed him for that matter.

People knew exactly where they stood with him. Jesus called the Scribes and Pharisees *"a brood of vipers'* (Matthew 12:34; 23:33 NKJV). However, he did withhold information when he knew it could not be processed correctly at the time. Or, if revealed prematurely, would give occasion to the enemy to destroy or hinder the work. For example, in his final discourse with his co-leaders, Jesus had much more he wanted to reveal to them. But he chose to withhold it until the Holy Spirit could prepare their hearts to receive it. Jesus gave the critical information needed at the time—not information overload. He relied on the Holy Spirit to bring back information to their remembrance, to make sense of a situation, and to provide direction as to how to proceed.

Jesus also prepared his co-laborers for both positive and negative consequences. This equipped the disciples to not falter when scenarios did not unfold according to their desires, or pre-conceived plan. Jesus was candid in revealing that the supernatural work they were called to perform would be violently opposed. Despite the opposition, the Holy Spirit would guide them and protect them in the completion of the work. They were to be interdependently connected and in unity with the Spirit—not information dependent but Holy Spirit led.

"These things I have spoken to you, that you should not be made to stumble. They will put you out of the synagogues; yes, the time is coming that whoever kills you will think that he offers God service. And these things they will do to you because they have not known the Father nor Me. But these things I have told you, that when the time comes, you may remember that I told you of them. "And these things I did not say to you at the beginning, because I was with you.

"But now I go away to Him who sent Me, and none of you asks Me, 'Where are You going?' But because I have said these things to you, sorrow has filled your heart. Nevertheless I tell you the truth. It is to your advantage that I go away; for if I do not go away, the Helper will not come to you; but if I depart, I will send Him to you. And when He has come, He will convict the world of sin, and of righteousness, and of judgment: of sin, because they do not believe in Me; of righteousness, because I go to My Father and you see Me no more; of judgment, because the ruler of this world is judged.

"I still have many things to say to you, but you cannot bear them now. However, when He, the Spirit of truth, has come, He will guide you into all truth; for He will not speak on His own authority, but whatever He hears He will speak; and He will tell you things to come. He will glorify Me, for He will take of what is Mine and declare it to you. All things that the Father has are Mine. Therefore I said that He will take of Mine and declare it to you." (John 16:1-15 NKJV)

As master builders, while we are not solely dependent upon information, we *are* solidly grounded and *guided* by God's Word. From the outset of building the organization, all that is said and done must align with scriptural principles. This is the place of departure with much of what is being called "God's work" in the body of Christ. Works are being built according to the principles of the world. The church is infiltrated to such a degree, that many no longer recognize they are following the pattern of the world, not the blueprint of the kingdom. As a result, the work is fraught with competition, back-biting, in-fighting and every other evil work. As mentioned earlier, when a work is built according to the principles of the world, Satan has legal access to infiltrate it; these corruptive behaviors and practices are the inevitable result.

As a governing leader and master builder, whenever a corruptive practice or behavior is detected, it must be addressed forthrightly and quickly. If not, it will fester and act as a leaven and corrupt the entire work.

Guided by the light of his presence and Word, we build according to the pattern of the kingdom—the throne, which we covered in chapter three. As the governing leader and master builder, we must not deviate from the blueprint God has put into our spirit. His righteousness and justice must permeate the building process. We implement a kingdom government into the supernatural work.

Two criteria are essential in building with people from a kingdom governmental perspective. We must *create an environment that allows the Holy Spirit to move freely in and upon the people and co-laboring leaders*. This environment engenders the unity of the Spirit in which all feel included, valued and are meaningfully contributing to the work.

Practically, this means the master builders periodically assess where people are in the process. If feasible, the most effective method is to get "everyone in the room" and either do a formal (written) assessment or conduct a verbal discussion and document the feedback.

Unfortunately, most organizations do not follow through to the next step—*respond* to the articulated issues, needs, and suggestions for improvement (see *Epilogue* chapter for examples).

Secondly, we foster a *culture of honor*. We acknowledge where people *are*—possibly stuck or disengaged from the process. We value who they are as an individual, even though we may disagree with their idea or position. As Bethel senior pastor and author, Bill Johnson, aptly put it, "We recognize who a person is, without stumbling over who he is not."[1] Bethel Church in Redding, CA, has been a forerunner in the area of creating and sustaining a culture of honor.[2]

A culture of honor includes those elements that the organization agrees demonstrate respect and the value of the individual. These elements are based on biblical principles of how people will be treated in the organization. As illustration, a component of honor could be to demonstrate the willingness to listen to a person's ideas and provide a forum to express their ideas, without pre-judging or stifling their participation.

ARISE AND SHINE ANOINTING

Another aspect of light is the manifestation of God's light within us—the *eternal light*. As we approach the end of the age and God is forming his end-time army, Isaiah declares:

Arise, shine; For your light has come! And the glory of the LORD is risen upon you. For behold, the darkness shall cover the earth, and deep darkness the people; But the LORD will arise over you, And His glory will be seen upon you. (Isaiah 60:1-2 NKJV).

This light is God's glory manifesting in and through us. This anointing represents the fullness of the seven-fold Holy Spirit flowing through us as depicted in Isaiah 11:1-2 (NKJV):

*There shall come forth a Rod from the stem of Jesse, and a Branch shall grow out of his roots. The **Spirit of the LORD shall rest upon Him**, the Spirit of wisdom and understanding, the Spirit of counsel and might, the Spirit of knowledge and of the fear of the LORD (emphasis added).*

As governing leaders, we seek the fullness of the **Spirit Upon**, the *Mantle of Anointing for others* that allows us to flow in *wisdom and understanding, counsel and might, and knowledge and the fear of the Lord*; we are prepared to walk in the end-time ***Arise and Shine anointing***.

Isaiah 60:1-2 identifies what this anointing is—*the level of light of his glory increasing in you* such that people in the world (and the church in darkness), seek your counsel to solve problems. They want what you have for they *see* the glory (our spirits came from eternity so our spirit will recognize the eternal light when it sees it).

Chapter 61 of the book of Isaiah is a description of how this anointing functions.

The Spirit of the Sovereign Lord is upon me, for the Lord has anointed me to bring good news to the poor. He has sent me to comfort the broken hearted and to proclaim that captives will be released and prisoners will be freed. He has sent me to tell those who mourn that the time of the Lord's favor has come, and with it, the day of God's anger against their enemies. To all who mourn in Israel, he will give a crown of beauty for ashes, a joyous blessing instead of mourning, festive praise instead of despair. In their righteousness, they will be like great oaks that the Lord has planted for his own glory.

They will rebuild the ancient ruins, repairing cities destroyed long ago. They will revive them, though they have been deserted for many generations. Foreigners will be your servants. They will feed your flocks and plow your fields and tend your vineyards. ⁶ You will be called priests of the Lord, ministers of our God. You will feed on the treasures of the nations and boast in their riches. Instead of shame and dishonor, you will enjoy a double share of honor. You will possess a double portion of prosperity in your land, and everlasting joy will be yours.

"For I, the Lord, love justice. I hate robbery and wrongdoing. I will faithfully reward my people for their suffering and make an everlasting covenant with them. Their descendants will be recognized and honored among the nations. Everyone will realize that they are a people the Lord has blessed."

I am overwhelmed with joy in the Lord my God! For he has dressed me with the clothing of salvation and draped me in a robe of righteousness. I am like a bridegroom in his wedding suit or a bride with her jewels. The Sovereign Lord will show his justice to the nations of the world. Everyone will praise him! His righteousness will be like a garden in early spring, with plants springing up everywhere. (vs. 1-11NLT)

Verse 10 speaks of ***the Robe of Righteousness***—The Lord clothes us with this robe; he is our righteousness. The world and the darkened church, seek us out because all that we say and do is aligned with his righteousness. We love justice, therefore, we are able to judge righteously (using a Biblical standard). Jesus is seated on the throne; the foundation of his throne is righteousness and justice. *Psalm 97:2 (NLT): Clouds and darkness surround him;* ***Righteousness*** *and* ***justice*** *are the foundation of his throne* (emphasis added). The scripture also declares in *Psalm 37:6 (NKJV): He shall bring forth your* ***righteousness*** *as the light, and your* ***justice*** *as the noonday* (emphasis added).

As we align our life with the throne of God, the Lord says it will emit light; and all the resources of heaven are attracted to his throne. Therefore, they become available to us—they manifest in the earth. There is no lack in heaven. Therefore, on earth influence, wealth and material resources are attracted to us because of the throne. The caveat is that they manifest to serve his kingdom purposes not our personal aggrandizement.

As a governing leader, the manifestation of God's light through you is the reason why the work God calls you to will be fruitful in the midst of lack, even though the economy may be struggling.

The supernatural work is a call from the Lord to the end-time governing leaders as recorded in Ephesians 5:14-17 (NKJV):

*Therefore He says: "****Awake****, you who sleep,* ***Arise*** *from the dead, And Christ will give you* ***light****." See then that you walk circumspectly, not as fools but as wise, redeeming the time, because the days are evil. Therefore do not be unwise, but understand what the will of the Lord I (emphasis added).*

We are to **AWAKEN**—first ourselves, then the sleeping church. We are to *arise* from *dead (apathy, dead works)* into the light of our destiny. We are to be as the five wise virgins—Mat. 25:1-4 (NKJV) *"Then the kingdom of heaven shall be likened to ten virgins who took their lamps and went out to meet the bridegroom. Now five of them were wise, and five were foolish. Those who were foolish took their lamps and took no oil with them, but the wise took* *oil in their vessels with their lamps.* The wise virgins had the light and were watching and waiting, not distracted by the world, or works that will burn up as hay and stubble at the Judgment Seat. Their lights didn't go out; they kept the seven-fold Holy Spirit burning brightly within them. They are operating under the *Arise and Shine anointing*—they won't be caught off-guard at the bridegroom's arrival. They will have completed their assignment. They know what is going to happen and are prepared for it. They have searched the scriptures; they have heard the prophetic word and applied it to their lives—they are running their race to win!

The Lord admonishes us to walk wisely and understand what the will of the Lord is. To be circumspect is to be careful, diligent and prudent in all things. We are to be prepared for both the enemy's temptations and his snares. We are able to stand and weather his outright attacks and persecutions. This is what it means to know the *wiles* of the devil—his strategies to destroy you and ruin your testimony. *Put on the whole armor of God, that you may be able to stand against the **wiles** of the devil* (Eph. 6:7 NKJV, emphasis added). God says how we stand against these strategies is to use our military protection—the armor of God. We are in a war—the stakes are our eternal soul.

Open the Eyes of the Blind

Proverbs 8:28 (KJV) decrees, *"Where there is no vision, the people perish..."* In other words, the heavens must be opened to us in the prophetic dimension—through the revelatory word, visions and dreams, in such a way, that when the deliverer/forerunner receives the vision and divine blueprint, everyone catches it.

Since its inception, our Bible study (referenced in Chapter 5) has functioned as a supernatural work of God. Our vision is articulated in Daniel 11:32 (NKJV): *Those who do wickedly against the covenant he shall corrupt with flattery; but the people who know their God shall be strong, and carry out great exploits.* Our goal is to know our God, not know about him, but to encounter and experience him; and then to manifest his mighty power in great exploits in his Name. We believe Satan cannot corrupt us or deceive us, if we are aligned with the Word, and our hearts' desire is to pursue him for relationship. Based upon the foundation of the Word and our intimate relationship with Christ, will flow the mantle and anointing to do the work for which he has commissioned us —*Heal the sick, cleanse the lepers, raise the dead, cast out demons. Freely you have received, freely give* (Matthew 10:8 NKJV).

As we live and express that vision, God uses the prophetic dimension to help us internalize the vision more deeply. Individuals in the group "catch" the vision in their spirit and express prophetically what the Lord is presently "doing" to take us to the next level of the vision. For instance, God gave a revelatory word to an individual in our group that we should perform a prophetic act of nailing a "struggle" or a "secret sin" we were dealing with to the cross. His purpose was to reveal dark areas in our spirit that were hindering us from moving forward. As he made us aware, or we already had the awareness and had been releasing it to the Lord and then taking it back, he was in essence, *cleansing the lepers*. His objective is that "Satan have nothing in us" so that he can increase the manifestation of his presence in and through us, and therefore, his miracle-working power.

Staying prophetically connected is a means to keep the unity of the Spirit. We remain in the flow of the river of the Holy Spirit where God chooses who he is going to speak through, or provide guidance through dreams and visions. It creates a bond among the people; we are relationship-oriented rather than program-focused. We stay focused on and dependent upon the Holy Spirit, to lead and guide us in fulfilling his plan and purpose for our group.

An important point, as God reveals his plan to the deliverer/forerunner, how much and to whom the details of the plan are shared, is determined by the Lord. We should not automatically assume that all the details should be shared as they are revealed. The timing of releasing information is crucial, as many times the Lord will have the leader withhold details not to keep co-laborers in the dark, but rather the enemy. This will be illustrated in the next chapter as we look at one of the great master builders of the Bible—Nehemiah.

Free the Captives from Prison

From the outset of a supernatural work, we must understand that even though we seek those to co-labor with us that have surrendered their lives to the Lord, they will still have strongholds they have to overcome. The Lord brings individuals connected with the work into the knowledge of his Word and their gifts, as well as their part in the work. However, they are not "a completed work." We all carry baggage and bondages from which the Lord sets us free as we are ready—we come to the place of maturity and revelation to deal with it.

Transformation into the likeness of Christ is an ongoing process. Romans 12:2 identifies that the primary means by which we are transformed is through the renewing of our mind. *And do not be conformed to this world, but be transformed by the renewing of your mind, that you may prove what is that good and acceptable and perfect will of God* (NKJV). As we read and meditate on the scriptures on a daily basis, we are absorbing God's thoughts; we begin to filter our beliefs and structure our thought processes on the Word of God. As we interact with his Word, and allow the Holy Spirit to speak into our hearts, we begin to think and act from a kingdom perspective, not a worldly perspective.

Our actions flow from our thoughts; therefore, renewing the mind is an active process. Second Corinthians 10:5 instructs us that we are continually *"casting down arguments and every high thing that exalts itself against the knowledge of God, bringing every thought into captivity to the obedience of Christ"* (NKJV).

Transformation requires we walk in the fruit of the Spirit—*But the fruit of the Spirit is love, joy, peace, longsuffering, kindness, goodness, faithfulness, gentleness, self-control. Against such there is no law* (Galatians 5:22-23 NKJV). Our character is formed by the fruit of the Spirit and it is modeled in our words and actions.

A master builder fosters an environment that recognizes all are flawed, but views each person from God's perspective of who they are, "mighty men and women of valor." Like Gideon (see Judges 6:11), they may be hiding in the winepress captive to a spirit of fear or inadequacy, but God has called us as master builders to see beyond the visible into people's destiny. The only means to acquire this knowledge is to spend time with them. Get to know them—their hopes, dreams and struggles. For those co-laboring with us in the work, our role is to seek the Lord on their behalf and inquire, *"Father, what is in your heart for this individual?"*

In God's economy, people are not a "means to an end" they are the "end." He is concerned (and so should we) about every aspect of each individual contributing to the work. When an individual truly believes we care, it builds an environment of trust. In an atmosphere of trust and openness, eventually those things contrary to God's will in the person's life will surface.

As sins and struggles rise to the surface, things can get messy. If the person is willing to surrender and come into submission to the Word of God, we are to support him or her with prayer, and whatever resources are necessary to bring the individual into wholeness. In some instances, the person may have spiritual strongholds that require deliverance.

Releasing Those Who Sit in Dark Dungeons

Shipwreck happens in a supernatural work when we depend upon ourselves to build; we must continually build with God's heart. A master builder will guard against *dungeons*. Dungeons are mindsets of the world that are carried over into a supernatural work. These are accepted cultural beliefs and practices that have so infiltrated Christianity that we accept them and align our words and actions accordingly, even though they are contrary to the teaching of the Word of God.

An example of a cultural belief and practice is *diversity*. The principle of diversity is not found in the Bible. In fact, it is contrary to the Word of God. The word diversity is a derivative of *diverse*.[3] Synonyms of diverse are *separate, opposite, disparate, different, varied*, etc. According to the scriptures, when we come to Christ there are no distinctions among believers. *There is neither Jew nor Greek, there is neither slave nor free, there is neither male nor female; for you are all one in Christ Jesus* (Galatians 3:28 NKJV; see also Colossians 3:11).

Based on God's Word, if we focus on differences it will *separate* us. The implication of this is huge; we will not be able to come into unity with the Spirit because we are operating contrary to "oneness." The enemy is subtle; however, as master builders, we must be on guard against these mindsets infiltrating the work. We operate from a kingdom paradigm, not a world paradigm, no matter how entrenched it has become into the thinking of the church.

A dungeon can also be a *comfort zone* or a *territory*. An individual or group of individuals become territorial over an area of expertise, a way of doing things (a process or set of procedures), or the exercise of authority. They seek to maintain the current level of control and power they have attained by resisting change in these areas.

Individuals may seek to maintain the status quo. Their motive is related to their desire to remain in their *comfort zone*— staying in the same surroundings, doing the same things, at the same level. Master builders are routinely moving people *forward*—helping them overcome fear, complacency and the desire to *sit* in what they know rather than stepping out in faith. People get comfortable in the dungeon (what they know and what they did before) rather than where God is going—into the *new thing* where there is no template.

If we are building with God's heart, everyone in the work is *interdependent*—growing, connected, contributing at a meaningful level. They continue to move into new territory spiritually and experientially.

In the next chapter, Nehemiah provides us an historical example of a master builder living out these precepts.

Chapter 10

NEHEMIAH—MASTER BUILDER

The book of Nehemiah illustrates a practical example of God fulfilling a supernatural work through a master builder. Zerubbabel, the governor, and Ezra, the priest, were the initial deliverer/forerunners God sent to initiate the supernatural work of rebuilding Jerusalem. Nehemiah was chosen by God to build on the foundation laid by Zerubbabel and Ezra. His actions and behaviors throughout the building process, provide useful insights to all those called to a supernatural work.

Nehemiah, a devout Jew, held the position of cup bearer to Artexerxes of Babylon. He was an exile in a foreign land but God sovereignly placed him in a position of influence in the world of his day. We may be tempted to believe that in order to have a significant impact in God's plan and purposes, we must be in some sort of ministry position. Interestingly, Nehemiah, God's chosen deliverer/forerunner, held a secular job of great responsibility.

The book of Nehemiah is quite instructive for master builders. The events recorded begin eighteen years after Ezra the priest led the first group of Jewish exiles back to Jerusalem from Babylon. Nehemiah, anxious to know how the Jews in his homeland were faring, asked some travelers who had returned from Jerusalem for a report. When he learned of the inhabitants' deplorable condition and heard the walls of Jerusalem were broken down, he didn't throw up his hands in despair, or become incapacitated by fear. His response to the situation is recorded in Nehemiah 1:4 (NLT) *"When I heard this, I sat down and wept. In fact, for days I mourned, fasted and prayed to the God of heaven. . ."* Nehemiah grieved over the desolation and destruction, then fell to his knees and sought divine wisdom.

God chose a deliverer/forerunner whose heart could be touched with compassion and broken to the point of grief over the destruction of the walls. Nehemiah was able to enter into the Lord's suffering on behalf of the condition of the land and the spiritual state of the people. Like Jeremiah (31:16) and Jesus (John 11:35)—he wept.

CULTIVATING A RECEPTIVE, TENDER HEART

It is difficult to keep our hearts tender and receptive to the Lord's voice. Our tendency is to harden ourselves because of the continual onslaught of evil—unscrupulous secular and spiritual leaders, corrupt business practices, self-seeking lawmakers and lobbyists, and selfish, one-way relationships. However, the Lord seeks to and fro for an individual with his heart, to stand in the gap as his master builder. *"And I sought for a man among them, that should make up the hedge, and stand in the gap for me for the land, that I should not destroy it; but I found none"* (Ezekiel 22:30 KJV).

Note that Nehemiah not only grieved, he entered into fasting combined with intercession. This desire was placed in his heart by the Lord. God had already chosen Nehemiah and was drawing him to the work by initiating the hunger and yearning in his spirit. He took individual and family responsibility to repent of his own and his family's sins that contributed to and allowed the present situation. He reminded God of his faithfulness, reciting scriptural promises and claiming them in the current circumstances. Nehemiah used the same word given to a previous generation as an ongoing promise for the current situation.

Finally, he sought God on behalf of those who were faithful (maintaining spiritual discipline and listening for his voice), to give him favor with those in a position of human authority so that action could be taken. Moreover, he had already purposed in his heart to take action, but only that directed by the Spirit of God. Through repentance, intercession and prayer, a plan of action germinated in his spirit.

O Lord, God of heaven, the great and awesome God who keeps his covenant of unfailing love with those who love him and obey his commands, listen to my prayer! Look down and see me praying night and day for your people Israel. I confess that we have sinned against you. Yes, even my own family and I have sinned! We have sinned terribly by not obeying the commands, decrees, and regulations that you gave us through your servant Moses.

Please remember what you told your servant Moses: 'If you are unfaithful to me, I will scatter you among the nations. But if you return to me and obey my commands and live by them, then even if you are exiled to the ends of the earth, I will bring you back to the place I have chosen for my name to be honored.'

The people you rescued by your great power and strong hand are your servants. O Lord, please hear my prayer! Listen to the prayers of those of us who delight in honoring you. Please grant me success today by making the king favorable to me. Put it into his heart to be kind to me (Nehemiah 1:5-11 NLT).

HIDING THE PLAN IN OUR HEART

Nehemiah prayed through and received a detailed plan of requirements including a timeline from the Lord. Rather than prematurely setting the plan into motion, he waited for a sign of favor. It wasn't until the following spring (it was late autumn when he interceded and received the plan), that the Lord provided the open door of favor for Nehemiah to proceed. Nehemiah 2:1-2 (NLT) reads: *Early the following spring, in the month of Nisan, during the twentieth year of King Artaxerxes reign, I was serving the king his wine. I had never before appeared sad in his presence. So the king asked me, "Why are you looking so sad? You don't look sick to me. You must be deeply troubled.*

We in the western world have lost the impact of Nehemiah's statement that he *"appeared sad"* in the King's presence. In the Babylonian court of that day, for a servant, particularly a foreign-born servant, to express sadness in front of the king was reason enough to chop off his head! Perhaps the waiting was wearing on Nehemiah to the point of total discouragement. Was he fearful that it might already be too late to act? In the interim, was he worried the situation had deteriorated beyond hope? Or might he have begun to doubt, after this extended period, that the Lord would come through in response to his prayer? The text doesn't tell us; but, as humans, we have all been tempted by these thoughts when we have prayed, and believe we have received a plan in answer to our prayer, yet the situation continues to deteriorate while the opportunity to implement the answer hasn't yet materialized.

This is all common deliverer/forerunner preparation. God only cracks slightly the *door* we need *opened*; barely enough to take the initial step. This is our *death strip of faith* where we must stand on what God has revealed and not doubt in our hearts that the plan will come to fruition. In the background, he is preparing the way, so that in the fullness of time, the plan can unfold. As the Apostle Paul explained in Galatians 4:4-5 (NKJV), God waited for the appropriate time, when all things could unfold exactly as he had predetermined from the foundation of the world, to send us his Son. *But when the fullness of the time had come, God sent forth His Son, born of a woman, born under the law, to redeem those who were under the law, that we might receive the adoption as sons.* It's his timetable not ours.

Although the scriptures indicate Nehemiah was terrified, he boldly and succinctly told the king his problem. " . . . *How can I not be sad? For the city where my ancestors are buried is in ruins, and the gates have been destroyed by fire*" (Nehemiah 2:3 NLT).

In response, the king gave Nehemiah an affirmation of his favor, ". . . *Well how can I help you?* (Nehemiah 2:4 NLT). Because of his prior preparation, Nehemiah was able to provide a concrete and specific plan of action to the authority figure. He asked the king for two things: 1) authority to obtain the necessary cooperation and the release of resources to carry out the rebuilding activities; and 2) protection from theft and bodily harm.

When the day of opportunity arrived, Nehemiah was prepared. He had done his homework and had thoroughly thought out the dilemma. He requested only the absolute necessities to carry out the plan. Most importantly, he did not speak in generalities, his requirements were specific, and he clearly identified the parties from whom he needed cooperation (Nehemiah 2:7-9 NLT).

I also said to the king, "If it please the king let me have letters addressed to the governors of the province west of the Euphrates River, instructing them to let me travel safely through their territories on my way to Judah. And please give me a letter addressed to Asaph, the manager of the king's forest instructing him to give me timber. I will need it to make beams for the gates of the Temple fortress, for the city walls, and for a house for myself." And the king granted these requests, because the gracious hand of God was on me.

When I came to the governors of the province west of the Euphrates River, I delivered the king's letters to them. The king, I should add, had sent along army officers and horsemen to protect me.

At this point, Nehemiah journeyed to Jerusalem. He continued to divulge the plan only on a "need-to-know" basis. As master builders, we would do well to follow Nehemiah's example of implementing what God has laid on our heart. Nehemiah doesn't broadcast the Lord's plan to all those around him. Like Mary, mother of Jesus, he hid God's plan in his heart, and only revealed what was necessary to those whom the Holy Spirit directed.

. . . Three days later, I slipped out during the night, taking only a few others with me. I had not told anyone about the plans God had put in my heart for Jerusalem (Nehemiah 2:11-12 NLT).

Oftentimes, we give the enemy a place to attack and/or destroy the work of God by divulging the plan prematurely, before the Lord has set in place all that is necessary for its fulfillment. There is a set time or sequence of God's unfolding plan. As Exodus 9:5 (KJV) illustrates, *And the LORD appointed a **set time**, saying, tomorrow the LORD shall do this thing in the land* (emphasis added). We must follow the leading of the Holy Spirit. If we do not allow God to set the time, information may get into the hands of those in a position to block or oppose the work. We then may face unnecessary obstacles to the implementation of what God has laid on our heart. Timing is crucial. We must keep in our heart what the Lord has spoken until the appropriate time. Telling others prematurely, can set in motion actions and decisions contrary to the Lord's purposes.

EVERYONE CARRIES RESPONSIBILITY FOR THE WORK

While Nehemiah was selective in sharing the details of God's plan for rebuilding the walls, he did not take a "lone ranger" approach in delegating responsibility for the reconstruction. A good master builder recognizes that God uses the body of Christ to do his work and fulfill his purpose in the earth. He or she actively seeks co-laborers. Nehemiah did not operate as *a one man show*. Consequently, Nehemiah assigned a portion of the rebuilding of the wall to his co-laborers, particularly in the areas where they had a vested interest. For example, the scripture states in Nehemiah 3:28 (NLT) *Above the Horse Gate, the priests repaired the wall. Each one repaired the section immediately across from his own house.*

Accountability is an integral part of master builder leadership. The church in our age is in a *"do it for you"* or *"catering to you"* mode such that a few select people implement the work without the help or support of everyone. While many in leadership decry the non-commitment of the masses, much of it is self-imposed by not allowing meaningful contribution, or not assigning accountability and responsibility to all parts of the body.

IMPLICATIONS OF STARTING A SUPERNATURAL WORK

Just as in Nehemiah's case, when the supernatural work process starts, people *will* get upset and you *will* face persecution, censure and ridicule. From Genesis to Revelation, the Lord's servants have faced opposition in implementing a supernatural work. As a testimony that his church will ultimately succeed, Jesus said in Matthew 16:18 (NLT), *"Now I say to you that you are Peter (which means rock) and upon this rock I will build my church, and all the powers of hell will not conquer it."* However, Jesus also told his disciples *". . . Here on earth you will have many trials and sorrows. But take heart for I have overcome the world"* (John 16:33 NLT). And *". . . Since they persecuted me, naturally they will persecute you"* (John 15:20 NLT).

Opposition will Come

A master builder is to expect opposition, not be blindsided by it. Nehemiah's handling of opposition is exemplary. Initially, the opposition was external. In Chapter 4, verses 1-3 (NLT), the enemy used anger, mockery and intimidation.

> *Sanballat was very angry when he learned that we were rebuilding the wall. He flew into a rage and mocked the Jews, saying in front of his friends and the Samarian army officers, "What does this bunch of poor, feeble Jews think they are doing? Do they think they can build the wall in a single day by just offering a few sacrifices? Do they actually think they can make something of stones from a rubbish heap – and charred ones at that?*

> *Tobiah the Ammonite, who was standing beside him remarked, 'That stone wall would collapse if even a fox walked along the top of it!*

In the face of opposition, it is vital to remain in our spiritual authority, *For though we walk in the flesh, we do not war after the flesh. For the weapons of our warfare are not carnal but mighty through God to the pulling down of strongholds; Casting down imaginations, and every high thing that exalts itself against the knowledge of God and bringing into captivity every thought to the obedience of Christ* (2 Cor.10:3-5 NLT). People are not the enemy; they are merely following the dictates of the god of this world. We should expect, rather than be surprised by, their antagonism.

Nehemiah's response in verse 4 was to pray—not to argue, persuade or ridicule in return. *"Then I prayed, 'Hear us, our God, for we are being mocked'. . ."* (NLT). He correctly interprets his enemies' intent and asks the Lord to deal with them. He does not "get into the flesh" and attack his enemies or respond to their taunts. Moreover, Nehemiah does not internalize their comments even though they have some merit. They *are* a "rag-tag" group of individuals and they *have* re-used old, charred stones in their rebuilding. However, where crucial, God has provided new materials such as the timber for the gates, though Nehemiah wisely withholds that information. Surely, if their enemies were aware of the timber, they would seek to destroy it.

Nehemiah chose to stay close to the Lord and listen to *his* voice. He trusted the Lord to frustrate the strategies and plans of the enemy against him personally, and the work they were called to do. In the physical, he instructed the people to put on their armor in readiness to use their weapons at a moment's notice. *". . . I stationed the people to stand guard by families, armed with swords, spears and bows"* (Nehemiah 4:13 NLT).

While Nehemiah did not attack his enemies, he mentally, physically and spiritually prepared himself and the people. Spiritually, we put on God's armor and weapons to offensively stand against the enemy. Our weapons are the Name and the blood of Jesus, the Word of God, and the word of our testimony. Physically, we must do whatever is required to sensibly stay out of harm's way. We do not foolishly run into danger expecting the Lord's protection.

Nehemiah faced internal opposition as well. The Jews were hindering the work of God by taking advantage of the misfortune of others in their midst.

> *When I (Nehemiah) heard their complaints, I was very angry. After thinking it over, I spoke out against these nobles and officials. I told them, 'You are hurting your own relatives by charging interest when they borrow money!' Then I called a public meeting to deal with the problem. (Nehemiah 5:6-7 NLT)*

Notice Nehemiah did not allow internal dissension to go unchecked. When he was made aware of a problem, he dealt with it quickly and publicly. He did not allow Satan to get a foothold, and consequently, destroy the work of rebuilding from within.

Enemy Strategies of Intimidation and Accusation

We should not be ignorant of Satan's strategies. *Intimidation* and *accusation* are two of the most potent offensive strategies in the enemy's arsenal to stop the forward motion of a supernatural work. After all, Satan IS the accuser of the brethren (Job 1:6; Zech. 3:2 KJV).

We should not be surprised when working to restore unity, that we are accused of causing division. Naively, we may believe internal squabbling can be avoided rather than confronted. However, not everyone will be at the same level of spiritual maturity and character, therefore, discord and dissension are inevitable and must be addressed or they *will* destroy the building process. Similarly, if you stand immovable upon the Truth, you will be accused of fundamentalism, fanaticism or intolerance. Satan seeks to use the people you expect to stand and be unified with you, to intimidate you.

What is the *objective* of intimidation? Nehemiah answers that question in the sixth chapter. Note his response to his enemies' plot to kill him and their slanderous accusations in letters to governing authorities. *They were just trying to intimidate us, imagining that they could discourage us and stop the work. So I continued the work with even greater determination.* (Nehemiah 6:9 NLT). Nehemiah's response is devoid of fear, discouragement or retreat, rather he stood firm and persevered.

Nehemiah faced intimidation throughout the building process. He faced ridicule from external enemies that had a significant interest in maintaining their power and the status quo (chapter 4). He faced internal squabbling and personal financial hardship (Chapter 5). For example, *I (Nehemiah) asked for nothing, even though I regularly fed 150 Jewish officials at my table, besides all the visitors from other lands!* (Nehemiah 5:17 NLT). In the sixth chapter, he faced the threat of bodily harm from his enemies (6:2), together with deception and ungodly counsel from false prophets, who attempted to shift Nehemiah's focus to self-preservation in order to later accuse and discredit him. (Nehemiah 6:10-12 NLT).

> *Later I went to visit Shemaiah son of Delaiah and grandson of Mehetabel, who was confined to his home. He said, 'Let us meet together inside the Temple of God and bolt the doors shut. Your enemies are coming to kill you tonight. But I replied, 'Should someone in my position run from danger? Should someone in my position enter the Temple to save his life? No, I won't do it.' I realized that God had not spoken to him but that he had uttered this prophecy against me because Tobiah and Sanballat had hired him.*

CULTIVATING DISCERNMENT

Nehemiah demonstrated Spirit-led discernment in operationalizing his master builder role. Building requires "trust." Notwithstanding, Jesus cautioned his disciples to be ". . . *wise as serpents and harmless as doves*" (Matthew 10:16 KJV). In our relationships and associations throughout the building process, we cannot merely assume that those espousing alignment with the work are truly supporting it. If the enemy is thwarted in his outright attempts to destroy the work, he will seek to infiltrate and become a part of it. His objective is to destroy from within. Therefore, we can expect the enemy to seek out spies, double-minded believers and false prophets to infiltrate and infect the camp. Nehemiah was careful and prudent in matters of trust, ensuring that the individuals' walk matched their talk before putting confidence in them.

Throughout the building process, Nehemiah's discernment acted as a wall of protection, keeping the enemy without and corruption from gaining a foothold within.

POST-BUILDING

The most dangerous stage in the building process is "completion." If not careful, the master builder and co-laborers may let down their guard and begin to revel in success. Nehemiah, ever the vigilant master builder, modeled the way of righteousness for builders. He put God first. He believed and held fast to what God had spoken to him regardless of the opposition, and in spite of the obstacles, to fulfilling it. Upon completion of the *physical* walls, Nehemiah and his co-laborers realized the rebuilding of their *spiritual* walls was the *heart* of the whole process.

Celebration and Confession

Rather than resting on their laurels, the co-laborers followed Nehemiah's example and gave precedence to the Word of God in their completion celebration (Nehemiah 8:2-3 NLT).

> *So on October 8 Ezra the priest brought the Book of the Law before the assembly, which included the men and women and all the children old enough to understand. He faced the square just inside the Water Gate from early morning until noon and read aloud to everyone who could understand. All the people listened closely to the Book of the Law.*

As the law was read, the conviction of the Holy Spirit fell on the people for the text says "*. . . they had been weeping as they listened to the words of the law*" (Nehemiah 8:9 NLT). Nehemiah, however, instructed them to continue to praise and worship the Lord in sacred celebration of the day. Nehemiah wisely understood that the people needed an extended time of worship and praise to experience the Lord's goodness and re-establish their relationship with him. They had repaired the physical walls of Jerusalem, now the Lord would expose the broken down spiritual condition of their hearts that led to the destruction in the first place.

The following day, the people assembled to hear the Word. The conviction of the Holy Spirit had time to work in their hearts. They began with *confession* of their sins and those of their ancestors (Nehemiah 9:2 NLT). Believers today need a greater understanding of what these Judeans clearly grasped, God is *holy* and sin cannot enter his presence. Sin must be judged. God desires to tabernacle with us, but he cannot because of the sin in our camp. We presumptuously believe we can stand in his presence, yet live in disregard of his spiritual and moral law. That is simply not true; and therefore, God has withheld his presence from our midst, lest he judge us in accordance with his holiness.

As the Book of the Law was read, the people learned they had not been following God's commands. They had long neglected celebration of the Jewish feasts. These feasts were spiritual markers God had instituted to be reminders of his love and faithfulness to his covenant with them. God used the Feast of Tabernacles (Nehemiah 8:14) to call them back to a meaningful experience of his presence—an invitation to relationship in which he would again dwell among them.

In turn, the people humbled themselves and fasted; they renewed their commitment to the Lord by making vows in those areas they had been disobedient to the Word. They recorded them in a document (lest they forget their vows); then publicly, they swore an oath to fulfill the vows (Nehemiah 9 & 10).

The Lord has given us a pattern of a master builder in Nehemiah. He was called to both physical and spiritual building/rebuilding. To build collectively, certain spiritual outcomes must be the focus: 1) recognition of areas where we are not in *obedience* to the Word; 2) the acknowledgment of areas of our failing (repentance); and 3) making the appropriate vows (commitments) to *maintain* what has been built. The ultimate outcome is the deepening of our intimate relationship with God. What has been built must become a "spiritual marker" that we continue to commemorate, and periodically revisit, to evaluate the stability of the supernatural work.

Chapter 11

CHARGE AND CHANGE THE ATMOSPHERE

Master builder Nehemiah illustrated that one cannot be complacent about the atmosphere. Nehemiah actively controlled the atmosphere through prayer and speaking the Word of God. He upheld God's logos and rhema Word in the face of opposition. He spiritually discerned and actively resisted the intimidation of those under demonic influence. Nehemiah came against dissension in the camp, bringing issues and problems to a quick resolution by righteous judgment.

According to Webster's online dictionary, an *atmosphere*[1] is a surrounding influence or environment. As believers, we know that an atmosphere can be influenced demonically, or by the Holy Spirit. Currently, much of the atmosphere is influenced by demonic activity. It is as though Spirit-filled believers have abdicated their responsibility to take authority in the spirit realm.

Complacency can open the door to the enemy. An improper biblical foundation can cause us to vacillate in our beliefs and focus on our own interests rather than Christ's. If we lack the understanding of our position in Christ, we cannot act with his authority in the earth. Together, these allow the enemy a foothold in our lives and it will infiltrate the supernatural work.

DECEPTION AND COMPROMISE

Historically, the enemy uses the same strategies with every generation. Among the favorites in his arsenal are *deception* and *compromise*. In the last days, Jesus warned that deception would be so widespread, through false messiahs and false prophets, that the very elect could be deceived (Matthew 24:24-25 KJV). The English word *deceived* is from the Greek *plana*[2] which means to cause to roam from safety, truth, or virtue. *The only protection against deception is to maintain an intimate relationship with Christ; and an unwavering commitment to the absolute authority of his Word.*

Paul warned believers in 2 Thessalonians 2:9-12 (NLT) that prior to the Lord's second coming, when the man of lawlessness is revealed (the Antichrist), a spirit of deception will cause people to believe the lies of the enemy. *This man will come to do the work of Satan with counterfeit power and signs and miracles. He will use every kind of evil deception to fool those on their way to destruction, because they refuse to love and accept the truth that would save them. So God will cause them to be greatly deceived, and they will believe these lies. Then they will be condemned for enjoying evil rather than believing the truth.*

The enemy is quite subtle and the deception is not initially blatant. It is contingent upon a deliver/forerunner that he or she offensively guards the atmosphere, so as to give no opening in the hedge of protection around the supernatural work. Satan's goal is to cause us to begin to *compromise truth* for comfort, pleasure, acceptance or tolerance. This is the very reason we shun calling sin a sin. Instead, we tolerate fornication, greed, self-absorption, pride and worldly ambition in order not to "offend" people. We would rather offend God than uphold the Truth. These actions and characteristics are a stench in the nostrils of a Holy God. They set both the believer and unbeliever on the path of destruction. The scripture is clear, if we are not continually living in the power of the Holy Spirit, we can be overcome by these sins. Paul clearly forewarned the believers in Galatians 5:19-21 (NLT) that to practice ongoing compromise—to indulge the flesh, is to forfeit the Kingdom of God. The danger is not only the failure of a supernatural work, but our own souls!

When you follow the desires of your sinful nature, the results are very clear: sexual immorality, impurity, lustful pleasures, idolatry, sorcery, hostility, quarreling, jealousy, outbursts of anger, selfish ambition, dissension, division, envy, drunkenness, wild parties and other sins like these. Let me tell you again, as I have done before, that anyone living that sort of life will not inherit the Kingdom of God.

We have roamed so far from *the* Truth that we actually boast of our ambition. Ministers of the gospel jealously compete with each other for sheep, counting their numbers as though that were an indication of kingdom success. Leaders and co-laborers must deal severely with their hearts in this area. Sins that God says he *hates*, we indulge in without the slightest conviction:

There are six things the Lord hates – no seven things he detests: haughty eyes, a lying tongue, hands that kill the innocent, a heart that plots evil, feet that race to do wrong, a false witness who pours out lies, a person who sows discord in a family, (Proverbs 6:16-19 NLT).

For example, lying is rampant even in the body of believers. How many times have you or someone you know committed to an activity, and at the last minute, gave a flimsy excuse to not participate, or just didn't show up at all? God hates lying; our word should be our bond. Others must be able to count on us to keep our word (Note: the Lord mentions lying twice!). Lying is deadly to a supernatural work. We must uphold a culture of honor and build our organization on truth, even when it hurts, and is not to our advantage to speak the truth.

The apostle Paul warned of the degree of deterioration in the spiritual condition of believers in the last days:

You should know this, Timothy, that in the last days there will be very difficult times. People will love only themselves and their money. They will be boastful and proud, scoffing at God, disobedient to their parents, and ungrateful. They will consider nothing sacred. They will be unloving and unforgiving; they will slander others and have no self-control. They will be cruel and hate what is good. They will betray their friends and be reckless, be puffed up with pride and love pleasure rather than God. They will act religious but they will reject the power that could make them godly. Stay away from people like that! (2 Timothy 3:1-5 NLT).

Paul was *not* referring to people in the world, he clearly stated they will act religious—claim Christ as their Lord and Savior. However, the power of the Holy Spirit is not operating in their lives. Their minds are still worldly, and their behaviors and deeds are still controlled by their flesh.

To maintain a Holy Spirit influenced atmosphere, requires that a deliverer/forerunner inspect his/her own spiritual condition using the criteria Paul described. Are we consumed by our own interests and problems? Is our career and the pursuit of wealth our primary ambition? Are we overly indulgent parents whose children are disobedient and ungrateful? Are we not allowing them to experience the consequences of their behavior? Have we adopted the world's standards in dress and acceptable behavior? Do the materials we read and view reflect the world's thinking and belief system? Do we believe and stand up for what the scripture calls good and evil? Or, are we politically correct, so as to please people, or not offend them? Are we loyal to our friends, or do our friendships depend upon their current usefulness to us? Are we proud of our status and accomplishments in the world or ministry such that we think we are better than others in our abilities and/or devotion? Is our focus a "comfortable" life rather than a sacrificial offering poured out to the Lord?

We, as deliverers/forerunners, assess ourselves along these criteria as well as our co-laborers self-assess. The second step is that we assess each other. The caveat is that we will all fall short in some area; however, the question is: *Are we willing to address it?* This is a scriptural command. *Confess your faults one to another, and pray one for another, that ye may be healed. The effectual fervent prayer of a righteous man availeth much,* (James 5:16 KJV). We must be willing to admit our faults. Secondly, allow the Holy Spirit to work with us—to correct us or inform us (if we do not have the proper understanding). In this manner, we stay in alignment with the supernatural work. Satan will not be able to infiltrate the work, because the "point of entrance" has been closed.

We are all flawed, and can remain blinded to a number of our flaws, until the Holy Spirit shines his light on them. When he does, then we must cooperate with him, not deny, blame or reject the truth. We, as leaders and co-laborers, come along side that person to help them address the heart issue that is at the root. The individual cannot just deal with the manifestations of the flaw. Kingdom confrontation is not about behavior modification, but change of heart.

Similarly, if a governing leader or co-laborer refuses to admit and address a fault in these areas, then the scripture admonishes us to depart from that person. *Be not deceived: evil communications corrupt good manners,* (1Corinthians 15:33 KJV). In other words, they are no longer to remain a part of the supernatural work. However, this is the last resort after every avenue of restoration is exhausted.

This process is one means through which we implement the throne of God into the organization. Immovable biblical principles are made visible in the lives of the leaders and co-laborers. We are governing according to righteousness and implementing his judgments. This is what keeps the unity of the Spirit; we are not focused on unity with each other. Man-focused unity tempts us to compromise or tolerate behaviors, attitudes and actions that are not biblical in order to keep unity among people.

PRESSURE THAT EXCEEDS THE ABILITY TO WITHSTAND

If a deliverer/forerunner is not watchful, pressure can overtake him or her in the form of adversity or continual, sustained stress. In the building process, we may experience financial setback, sickness, relationship problems, project issues or a myriad of other difficulties; these problems are common to man. If we are not careful, we can be tempted to sink into depression, self-pity and unbelief. Paul stressed to the Corinthians (1 Cor.10:13 NLT) *The temptations in your life are no different from what others experience. And God is faithful he will not allow the temptation to be more than you can stand. When you are tempted he will show you a way out so you can endure.*

How do we endure? Paul admonished the believers in Ephesians, in order to be strong in the Lord and in his power, we must put on the full armor of God (Eph. 6:10-11). During periods of intense adversity and stress, we often resort to relying on the flesh and our intellect to deal with our problems. If the enemy can lead us down this path, he will win the battle because the war is spiritual and cannot be won in the flesh. Moses succumbed to the flesh in attacking the Egyptian and killing him, as well as striking the rock in the desert; instead of speaking to it, as God had commanded him.

Paul pointed out this truth to the Ephesians (6:12 NLT), *For we are not fighting against flesh-and-blood enemies, but against evil rulers and authorities of the unseen world, against mighty powers in this dark world, and against evil spirits in heavenly places.* Paul clearly defined our armor, and emphasized that *each piece* must be put on in order to be spiritually protected.

> *Therefore put on every piece of God's armor so you will be able to resist the enemy in the time of evil. Then after the battle you will still be standing firm. Stand your ground, putting on the belt of truth and the body armor of God's righteousness. For shoes, put on the peace that comes from the Good News so that you will be fully prepared. In addition to all of these, hold up the shield of faith to stop the fiery arrows of the devil. Put on salvation as your helmet and take the sword of the Spirit, which is the word of God, (Ephesians 6:13-17 NLT).*

The point is that we must put on our armor *before* the battle. Have you ever seen a soldier go into battle without his weapons, or lacking combat protection? Of course not! Yet, we, as deliverers/forerunners, do not begin seeking the Lord in his Word, pray for his direction, or try to appropriate our faith until *after* we have tried every option in the flesh to deal with the situation. In the heat of the battle is not the time to dress ourselves in the armor. Oftentimes, when we finally put on our spiritual armor, the enemy already has a foothold, and we succumb to his strategy of destruction in the situation. We suffer the full impact of the problem we are facing, and consequently, our faith and trust may be crushed in the process. Then we blame the Lord for not coming through for us!

One of our most powerful weapons according to Paul is to "pray in the Spirit at all times and on every occasion. *Stay alert and persistent in your prayers for all believers everywhere,* (Ephesians 6:18 NLT).

During periods of extreme adversity and/or prolonged stress, our minds can become so overtaxed that we cannot think or reason clearly. Notwithstanding, God has provided our heavenly prayer language so that the Holy Spirit in us can speak Spirit-to-Spirit with the heart of God. Romans 8:26-28 (NLT) assures us that:

And the Holy Spirit helps us in our weakness. For example, we don't know what God wants us to pray for. But the Holy Spirit prays for us with groanings that cannot be expressed in words. And the Father who knows all hearts knows what the Spirit is saying, for the Spirit pleads for us believers in harmony with God's own will. And we know that God causes everything to work together for the good of those who love God and are called according to his purpose for them.

The upshot is that we must be fully armored on a daily basis. Otherwise, a breach in our spiritual walls is inevitable. The resulting chinks in our armor, will render us defenseless in the day of adversity.

STAY IN THE HIGH CALLING

To remain in the high calling where God can bless and release his anointing, power and presence, we must control the atmosphere by staying in our authority. Standing in our authority changes the spiritual climate from oppression to freedom. 1 Samuel 15:20-23 (NLT) provides a glimpse of the prophet and priest, Samuel's ability to stay in his authority.

"But I did obey the Lord," Saul insisted. "I carried out the mission he gave me. I brought back King Agag, but I destroyed everyone else. Then my troops brought in the best of the sheep, goats, cattle, and plunder to sacrifice to the Lord your God in Gilgal."

But Samuel replied, "What is more pleasing to the Lord: your burnt offerings and sacrifices or your obedience to his voice? Listen! Obedience is better than sacrifice, and submission is better than offering the fat of rams. Rebellion is as sinful as witchcraft, and stubbornness as bad as worshiping idols. So because you have rejected the command of the Lord, he has rejected you as king."

To protect authority means we must confront when necessary. If evil—corrupt behaviors and injustices are ignored, they become stronger. If you do not stand in your authority, Satan has a legal right to usurp it. Any occasion in which we abdicate our biblical authority, the enemy will use it against us. He has only as much authority as we allow him. Jesus said, *"Behold, I give you the authority to trample on serpents and scorpions, and over all the power of the enemy, and nothing shall by any means hurt you"* (Luke 10:19 NKJV). Standing in our authority ensures divine order. God is a God of order and works through God-given authority. We allow ourselves to be stripped of our spiritual authority when we operate out of the fear of man, rather than the fear of God.

Positive Affirmations

From the onset of the building process, an offensive strategy for taking over the atmosphere is to practice positive affirmation. Positive affirmations are statements of the future state of a situation or person, not the current status. Positive affirmations will express our faith and motivate people to move forward particularly in times of stress.

Positive affirmations honor God. They continue to confirm his Word. As we speak them into the atmosphere, we are calling for those things we cannot "see" in the natural yet. *(As it is written, I have made thee a father of many nations,) before him whom he believed, even God, who quickeneth the dead, and calleth those things which be not as though they were* (Romans 4:17 KJV). The practice of affirming others through supportive messages strengthens our faith to believe for the reality of what we are speaking. For example, when the Lord found Gideon hiding in the winepress he affirmed him by calling him a "mighty man of valor," not a sniveling coward!

Positive affirmations are biblically based. Scripture declares: *You are snared with the words of your lips, you are caught by the speech of your mouth* (Proverbs 6:2 AMP). If we speak negatively over a situation or person, those words have power to obstruct the flow and work of the Holy Spirit. Our negative words permeate the atmosphere with a negative future. The enemy will use the negative power of what was spoken to rob, kill and destroy, thereby, bringing the destructive word to fruition in the life of the person or situation.

If we put *commanding prayer* into practice it will result in an environment of positive affirmation because we are speaking to *"those things which do not exist as though they did"* (Romans 4:17 NKJV). Our mouth is affirming the Word of God and his creation, therefore, what we speak is blessed of God and will prosper.

As simplistic as it may sound, affirming messages have a tremendous impact upon individuals and organizations. They promote an atmosphere in which the *unity of the Spirit* can manifest. Individuals feel safe to experiment and "push the envelope" of their God-given potential and gifting.

CHARGE THE ATMOSPHERE

How do we charge the atmosphere with God's presence? We acknowledge him and speak his Name into the atmosphere. A supernatural work of God is founded and sustained through worship. Worship should be integral to every activity in the organization. On a regular basis, all members of the work should engage in extended periods of worship. It is contingent upon leadership to provide these times of worship so the Spirit of the Lord can permeate the work. He will speak to guide, direct and provide times of refreshing in his presence.

How we enter the Lord's presence is through praise and thanksgiving. We praise him for whom he is—creator, sustainer, and provider. He is everything we need, and so much bigger than any problem or obstacle the enemy can throw at us. Unfortunately, many believers view Satan as more powerful than God. Our culture is permeated with the occult and demonic. In essence, we have allowed the enemy to take over the atmosphere. We must stand in our authority as believers and take it back! Worship helps everyone engaged in the work to regain their perspective, particularly after a disappointment, or when facing a roadblock that appears insurmountable.

As we worship, we acknowledge our total dependency on him and profess his sovereignty over our lives and every situation. In this environment of surrender, the Holy Spirit can move freely on the hearts of the people. Remember God is concerned about our heart not our abilities. As governing leaders, it is our responsibility to facilitate an environment in which God's presence permeates the atmosphere.

Pastor and author Bill Johnson in his book *Face to Face* stated, "We become what we worship,"[3] a simple statement but utterly profound. If we worship God in the beauty of his holiness, we in turn, become more holy like him. Whatever captivates our heart is what we worship. That is why it is vital to guard our heart. Worship guards our heart as we surrender it to him.

The Structure of the Heavens

The term "supernatural" suggests something that is beyond the natural. To be supernatural is to be seated in the heavenly realms. The term "seated in heavenly realms" means we are operating from eternity in our spirit, not in the flesh. We are wielding our God-appointed authority and taking an offensive stance against the enemy. In Ephesians 2:2 (KJV), Satan is referred to as *"the prince, the power of the air, the spirit that now worketh in the children of disobedience."*

Satan's location is the *second* heaven—the *unseen realm*. His kingdom is situated in this realm and is structured by rank and authority. *For we do not wrestle against flesh and blood, but against principalities, against powers, against the rulers of the darkness of this age, against spiritual hosts of wickedness in the heavenly places,* (Ephesians 6:12, NKJV). The earth, sky, planets, universe are the *first* heaven. Man has authority under God in the first heaven. *Satan usurps authority whenever man abdicates his spiritual authority in this realm.*

In the second heaven, the unseen realm, God's heavenly host—the archangels, angelic host and guardian angels worship the Lord, give service and perform God's word. Michael, the archangel oversees principalities. He is the warrior angel (see Daniel 8-10; Rev. 12:7 & Jude 1:14). In Daniel 10:13, Michael was dispatched to fight the ruling spirit of Persia so that the messenger angel could pass through the second heaven to earth with the answer to Daniel's prayer.

The archangel Gabriel oversees ministry and is referred to as a messenger angel (see Luke 1:19; Luke 1:26 & 1Thes. 4:16). Of the angelic host—angels are assigned to churches (see Rev. 1:20; Rev. 2 & 3). Guardian angels perform protective ministry such as the angel that appeared to Peter in prison instructing Peter to follow him. Peter's chains supernaturally fell off and he was guided out of prison past two guards who did not "see" him, and through the iron gates which automatically opened. Then the angel departed from him (see Acts 12:5-10).

Satan's rank and authority mimics God's rank and authority of the heavenly host. The highest ranks of the demonic hosts are principalities. *Principalities* rule over nations; ruling *spirits* over states, cities or regions (e.g., in Daniel 10:13, the messenger angel encountered ruling spirits over different regions of Persia; therefore, the archangel Michael was sent to fight the ruling principality of the kingdom of Persia; Michael had to knock out the top-dog). The *rulers of darkness* are generals in Satan's army; while the *hosts of wickedness are* demons who obey the generals' commands.

The *third* heaven is where God dwells (see 2 Cor. 12:1, 2 & 4; Rev 4:1-2). God's throne room is in this realm. *Seraphim* (Isaiah, 6:1-3 & Rev. 4:8-11), called the *burning ones,* oversee worship in the heavenly throne room. They are the third heaven's highest-ranking angels. They have six wings and are full of eyes in front and back. *Cherubim* (Ezekiel 10:12, 18-19) are the angels surrounding God's throne. They cover and protect the glory. They also function as celestial chariots that carry the glory of God, and are found wherever the *Shekinah Glory* manifests. Cherubim are covered with precious stones of varied colors; they have four faces and four wings with the likeness of a man's hand under each wing. The four faces are an ox, lion, eagle and man.

To manifest a supernatural work in the earth will incite the demonic kingdom in the *second heaven* to war against it, for it is a supernatural work that takes ground from the enemy to establish the Kingdom of God in the earth.

In the next chapter, we will cover how to war in the heavenlies. It is in the spiritual realm that the battle is won, not fighting in the natural, people and obstacles. Every earth-birthed strategy will fail, as carnal reasoning and weapons do not work in a spiritual realm. *For the weapons of our warfare are not carnal, but mighty through God to the pulling down of strong holds* (2 Cor. 10:4 KJV).

Chapter 12

WARFARE WORSHIP

In this season, a new form of worship is emerging—warfare worship. God is working in the hearts of his people to worship as warriors, as he is revealing himself as a warrior. *But the Lord stands beside me like a great warrior. Before him my persecutors will stumble. They cannot defeat me. They will fail and be thoroughly humiliated. Their dishonor will never be forgotten* (Jeremiah 20:11 NLT).

WARFARE WORSHIP

Our revelation of God, and what he is doing, must never remain static. We are ever-increasing in our knowledge and experience of him. We are in perpetual motion with him as he moves us forward in the spiritual realm—into the new and the deeper realms of his hidden mysteries and glory.

This deeper realm of penetration of the glory has not escaped Satan's notice. He and his demonic host are at war with the saints. They particularly target—to rob, kill and destroy those who manifest the Light that exposes their dark, evil works. Consequently, the Lord is calling his governing leaders of his supernatural works in the earth, to rise up as generals and teach the people to be warriors.

We, as a body, are still caught up in the Lord's first coming—as savior—meek and mild; however, He is coming again, this time with a sword as King of Kings and Lord of Lords.

> *And I saw heaven opened, and behold a white horse; and he that sat upon him was called Faithful and True, and in righteousness he doth judge and make war. His eyes were as a flame of fire, and on his head were many crowns; and he had a name written, that no man knew, but he himself. And he was clothed with a vesture dipped in blood: and his name is called The Word of God. And the armies which were in heaven followed him upon white horses, clothed in fine linen, white and clean. And out of his mouth goeth a sharp sword, that with it he should smite the nations: and he shall rule them with a rod of iron: and he treadeth the winepress of the fierceness and wrath of Almighty God. And he hath on his vesture and on his thigh a name written, KING OF KINGS, AND LORD OF LORDS, (Revelation 19:11-16 KJV).*

Jesus is a warrior. His first coming was to bring salvation to the earth through his death on the cross and his resurrection to everlasting life. Ironically, the Jews misinterpreted the Messiah's mission when he came into the world. They were looking for a warrior and king and didn't recognize him as the suffering servant who had come to redeem them from sin. He conquered sin and death—the two chains with which we were bound to Satan's rule and reign. He opened the heavens to us; we have access through Jesus to the Father and all the riches of glory. He was a conqueror but not in the way they expected! Christ's work is finished. We must appropriate or enact the authority that Jesus has given us through the power of the Holy Spirit, working in and through us. Let us not fall prey to the same misidentification of Jesus in our age.

Much of the body of Christ appears stagnant in their revelation of Jesus. It is one-sided. We behold him as redeemer, but we have not fully entered into the revelation of Christ as warrior. Believers face the same danger as the Jews in the time of Christ. Our expectations are based on the revelation to a previous generation. However, God has a broader revelation for these days.

As governing leaders, our mandate is to move into this fuller revelation of warrior. God is preparing his army. Governing leaders are the generals in this army. Therefore, those called to lead supernatural works, should be in the forefront of teaching co-leaders and supporters of the work to war. As David recorded in the Psalms, *He teaches my hands to make war, so that my arms can bend a bow of bronze* (Psalm 18:34 NKJV). David is not speaking only of the physical but of the spiritual realm. David inquired of the Lord. He sought a heavenly strategy for battle; he did not devise his own plan. *David inquired of the LORD, saying, "Shall I pursue this troop? Shall I overtake them?" And He answered him, "Pursue, for you shall surely overtake them and without fail recover all."* (1 Samuel 30:8 NKJV). David's first strategy for war was prayer. The Psalms record his prayers. Again and again, he petitioned the Lord to destroy His enemies. He realized the real battle was not with flesh and blood, but with the demonic realm that perpetrated the evil and wickedness. *Let God arise, Let His enemies be scattered; Let those also who hate Him flee before Him* (Psalm 68:1 NKJV). David also understood that God was his protection as he battled against the demonic realm to secure Israel's inheritance. *For You have been a shelter for me, A strong tower from the enemy* (Psalm 61:3 NKJV).

Speaking Destiny

The so called "boomer generation," for the most part, failed to speak forth their destiny and that of their children and future generations. The lack of prophetic utterance into the atmosphere of God's plan and purpose over us, and our children, created a vacuum in the atmosphere. In the absence of God's people proclaiming the prophetic destiny of their generation and that of their children's, Satan filled the void. Any time God's people abdicate their responsibility and authority the enemy will usurp it!

Consequently, Satan has permeated the atmosphere with the demonic. For instance, when the boomer generation forfeited their watch over the schools, God and prayer were eliminated. The enemy gained a foothold. Bullying has so infiltrated our schools that children are taking their own lives because of it. This was unheard of a generation ago! Moreover, children are bringing guns to school and killing classmates and faculty.

In the vacuum, Satan has created the perception that he is bigger than God. The current generation has grown up with a better understanding of the demonic than of God. Consider the perception-creating capacity of the *Twilight* movies and the *Harry Potter* series that have indoctrinated an entire generation into witchcraft! A cultural phenomenon of perceiving a dark shadow following oneself is widely reported by the younger generation—Christian and non-Christian!

It should not be surprising, that in this season, the Lord is revealing himself as a warrior. In retrospect, we understand why Satan created the counter-culture movement of the 1960's, with its drug-crazed *hippies*, decrying war and proffering the enemy's false peace movement. It was all about love, free love—unconditional, with no responsibility or concern for the other's welfare. Sound familiar? It is the same definition of love attributed to Jesus in our day—unconditional with no repentance. Much of the body of Christ has deteriorated into the same deplorable condition of the hippies of the 60's—they have no desire to war. Many are deceived that there is no hope, and that Satan's perpetration of evil is greater than God's capacity to overthrow him.

Despite our latent understanding, God has called us to speak both our destiny and that of future generations into the atmosphere. We must begin now! We can halt the tsunami of evil overwhelming the younger and future generations. We can no longer sit idly, watching the enemy rob our children of a future. Our assignment is to immobilize his lies, his intimidation and oppression—that demands warfare!

Possibly you are wondering, how a supernatural work is connected to speaking destiny over future generations. They are divinely intertwined. As we spoke earlier, a mantle stays with a mission. While we are the governing generation, our mantle will pass to the next generation. Fortunately, most young people are aware they are in a battle. For example, note the worship songs coming forth in this season. They are centered on two themes, warfare and a deeper revelation of heaven—the glory and holiness of God. Satan knows his time is short, to survive the oncoming, onslaught of evil, it is imperative we learn how to war from heavenly places.

In the face of a sustained, full frontal assault of the enemy, we may become weary and despondent as did the prophet Jeremiah. God continued to give him messages of judgment to pronounce over the nation of Israel and the people despised him. They began persecuting Jeremiah and it appeared to Jeremiah that the Lord was not helping him. At this juncture, the Lord reminded Jeremiah he was to influence the people, not be influenced *by* them. This is a crucial point. *We are to displace the powers of darkness; they are not to trample on us.*

> *Then I said,*
> *"Lord, you know what's happening to me. Please step in and help me. Punish my persecutors! Please give me time; don't let me die young. It's for your sake that I am suffering. When I discovered your words, I devoured them. They are my joy and my heart's delight, for I bear your name, O Lord God of Heaven's Armies. I never joined the people in their merry feasts. I sat alone because your hand was on me. I was filled with indignation at their sins. Why then does my suffering continue? Why is my wound so incurable? Your help seems as uncertain as a seasonal brook, like a spring that has gone dry."*

> *This is how the Lord responds:*
> *"If you return to me, I will restore you so you can continue to serve me. If you speak good words rather than worthless ones, you will be my spokesman. You must influence them; do not let them influence you! They will fight against you like an attacking army, but I will make you as secure as a fortified wall of bronze. They will not conquer you, for I am with you to protect and rescue you. I, the Lord, have spoken! Yes, I will certainly keep you safe from these wicked men. I will rescue you from their cruel hands,"* (Jeremiah 15:15-21 NLT).

To keep the battle in perspective, the Lord has *already won* the victory. Our part is to stand in faith appropriating the victory Christ has already won. How do we do this? First, we are established in our heart that our God is sovereign and all-powerful; no demonic force can stand against his will. Our assignment is to put into effect the victory Christ has already won over the powers of darkness. *And having spoiled principalities and powers, he made a shew of them openly, triumphing over them in it* (Colossians 2:15 KJV). When we know how *big* our God is, the size of our enemy becomes trivial. The prophet Jeremiah altered his perspective and received the revelation of God as a warrior. This enabled him to enter into the place of confidence and rest.

> *But the Lord stands beside me like a great warrior. Before him my persecutors will stumble. They cannot defeat me. They will fail and be*

thoroughly humiliated. Their dishonor will never be forgotten, (Jeremiah 20:11NLT).

Before entering into combat, we clothe ourselves with the armor of God detailed in Ephesians 6:13-17. Secondly, we follow *his* pattern for warfare. Judah's King Jehoshaphat provides a biblical illustration of how to engage in spiritual warfare. In 2 Chronicles, chapter 20, the armies of three neighboring nations declared war on Judah. Jehoshaphat, badly shaken by this news, called a national fast of repentance and intercession to the Lord. Jehoshaphat demonstrated confidence in God's ability to deliver the nation, not in his own military strength or ability to strategize.

Jehoshaphat stood before the community of Judah and Jerusalem in front of the new courtyard at the Temple of the Lord. He prayed, "O Lord, God of our ancestors, you alone are the God who is in heaven. You are ruler of all the kingdoms of the earth. You are powerful and mighty; no one can stand against you! O our God, did you not drive out those who lived in this land when your people Israel arrived? And did you not give this land forever to the descendants of your friend Abraham? Your people settled here and built this Temple to honor your name. They said, 'Whenever we are faced with any calamity such as war, plague, or famine, we can come to stand in your presence before this Temple where your name is honored. We can cry out to you to save us, and you will hear us and rescue us,' (2 Chronicles 20:5-9 NLT).

God responded to the nation's humility and dependence upon him. Through the prophet Jahaziel, the Lord revealed to the Israelites the battle plan of heaven. Their battle stance was not to fear the enemy or be paralyzed by the enemy's size, because the battle was the Lord's not theirs. They were to stand in their position of spiritual authority and not abdicate it! If we are overcome by a spirit of fear, we give the enemy an entrance point to attack us.

Further, the Israelites were to strike first even though they were heavily outnumbered. They were to take an *offensive* position, not sit back until they were attacked by the enemy. However, the Lord assured them they would *not* have to fight, just stand quietly and watch his deliverance operation. Moreover, the war would be fought through worship—the high praise of the worshippers would send out the heavenly host causing confusion in the enemies' camp turning their evil plan upon themselves.

As all the men of Judah stood before the Lord with their little ones, wives, and children, the Spirit of the Lord came upon one of the men standing there. His name was Jahaziel son of Zechariah, son of Benaiah, son of Jeiel, son of Mattaniah, a Levite who was a descendant of Asaph.

He said, "Listen, all you people of Judah and Jerusalem! Listen, King Jehoshaphat! This is what the Lord says: Do not be afraid! Don't be discouraged by this mighty army, for the battle is not yours, but God's. Tomorrow, march out against them. You will find them coming up through the ascent of Ziz at the end of the valley that opens into the wilderness of Jeruel. But you will not even need to fight. Take your positions; then stand still and watch the Lord's victory. He is with you, O people of Judah and Jerusalem. Do not be afraid or discouraged. Go out against them tomorrow, for the Lord is with you!"

Then King Jehoshaphat bowed low with his face to the ground. And all the people of Judah and Jerusalem did the same, worshiping the Lord. Then the Levites from the clans of Kohath and Korah stood to praise the Lord, the God of Israel, with a very loud shout.

Early the next morning the army of Judah went out into the wilderness of Tekoa. On the way Jehoshaphat stopped and said, "Listen to me, all you people of Judah and Jerusalem! Believe in the Lord your God, and you will be able to stand firm. Believe in his prophets, and you will succeed."

After consulting the people, the king appointed singers to walk ahead of the army, singing to the Lord and praising him for his holy splendor. This is what they sang:

"Give thanks to the Lord; his faithful love endures forever!"

At the very moment they began to sing and give praise, the Lord caused the armies of Ammon, Moab, and Mount Seir to start fighting among themselves. The armies of Moab and Ammon turned against their allies from Mount Seir and killed every one of them. After they had destroyed the army of Seir, they began attacking each other. So when the army of Judah arrived at the lookout point in the wilderness, all they saw were dead bodies lying on the ground as far as they could see. Not a single one of the enemy had escaped.

King Jehoshaphat and his men went out to gather the plunder. They found vast amounts of equipment, clothing, and other valuables – more than they could carry. There was so much plunder that it took them three days just to collect it all! (2 Chronicles 20:13-25 NLT).

Blueprint for Warfare Worship

The above illustration outlines the heavenly blueprint for warfare worship. We enter into warfare worship with our hearts established that God hears us; he is sovereign and he is more powerful than the opposition. *Listen! The Lord's arm is not too weak to save you, nor is his ear too deaf to hear you call*, (Isaiah 59:1 NLT). We are secure in our belief that God is good. *Give thanks to the Lord, for he is good! His faithful love endures forever*, (1 Chronicles 16:34 NLT). And that he is for us. . . .*If God is for us, who can ever be against us?* (Romans 8:31 NLT).

1. **Enter into Thanksgiving and Praise**

    As we stated in chapter 5 in the section *Patterns of Prayer*, thankfulness is the gateway into the Lord's presence. *Enter into His gates with thanksgiving, And into His courts with praise. Be thankful to Him, and bless His name* (Psalm 100:4 NKJV). Our objective in warfare worship is to enter into his presence—the heavenly throne room. God's protocol is that we must pass through the gates of thanksgiving and the courts of praise, before we can enter into the holy of holies of his presence.

2. **Seek His Counsel**

    We prevail in the outer courts in thanksgiving and praise for however long it takes to enter in. Our desire is his presence. The Spirit will direct the worship music. We have grown accustomed to upbeat or lovely, soft choruses; however, as we go deeper into our praise, anointed warfare songs can usher us into the place of warring in the spirit. This is the realm of the spirit where we enter into tongues and allow the Holy Spirit to utter that which aligns with the Lord's purpose in the situation.

    After we have warred in the Spirit, a release or breakthrough will emerge, and the Lord will reveal his counsel. He will give us his

Word to speak over the problem, situation or person. It may be a passage of scripture or a rhema word. If a rhema word is given, God always aligns it with scripture.

3. **Do the Word – Assume Your Battle Position**

When the Lord gives a word, we must *do* the Word that is given. For example, a friend together with Rose and me, entered into warfare worship over our friend's son. The young man was scheduled for a sentencing hearing that day on a very serious charge. As we praised and warred in the Spirit, the Lord broke through with the passage of scripture quoted above, 2 Chronicles 20:13-26. Immediately, we received that word and began to do it. The young man's mother sat in proxy and we decreed the scripture over her. We thanked the Lord for sending out the heavenly host to do battle over this young man bringing the enemy's plans into confusion. We spoke God's justice over the courtroom, and that the judge would rule according to divine justice balanced by God's mercy. The Spirit led each of us into a battle position. The mother of the young man began decreeing the Word of God into the atmosphere reading aloud the Psalms. Rose continued to praise God exalting his Name, power and authority over the situation. I, Jan, continued to intercede in the Spirit – praying in tongues for God to send out the heavenly host in the second heaven to displace the demonic host. We maintained our battle positions until we simultaneously received a release in the Spirit. The victory was enacted when the young man received mercy from the judge. Our friend's son received a sentence of lesser severity – an order of follow-up rehabilitation counseling, truly a miracle!

On another occasion during warfare worship in our Bible study, the Holy Spirit gave a member of the group, chapter 43 of Isaiah as a prophetic word. He also gave her the woman in the group for whom this scripture was intended. Additionally, the Holy Spirit identified two individuals who were to pray over the person, and a third, to decree the passage of scripture over her.

The woman was seated in the middle of the group. The scripture was decreed over her – God loved her; she was precious in his sight. As she walked through rivers of difficulty, they would not overwhelm her; and the fires of oppression would not burn her. He would make rivers in the desert places in her life. God was reassuring her of his love and that He understood what she was going through; however, the scripture also spoke of sin. One of the women chosen to pray began speaking the issue the Lord revealed in terms of an idol in the woman's life. This led to a session of deliverance, as an idol is a demonic stronghold. Afterward, the other individual prophetically decreed over the woman her destiny and the defeat of the enemy in her life. At this juncture, the woman received total breakthrough. We all praised the Lord and rejoiced.

A supernatural work of God is a target of the enemy. We must learn to war. The battle is fought in the heavenlies—the Holy Spirit guides and directs the battle and releases the Word over the situation. Our part is to learn how to enter into the heavenly realm of worship, so that we can receive the revelatory word; then we must do it!

Epilogue

CONCEPTS IN PRACTICE

Talking in theory always sounds good and all conditions are perfect in a hypothetical model. However, in the real world, *how are the biblical concepts in this book made visible and practical?* In the first example, we provide a macro-level view of the concepts at work through a city-wide clean-up project. The second illustration is a micro-level view of a specific element, conflict. The purpose of the second example is to demonstrate that conflict is inevitable; it must not be suppressed but dealt with.

The following clean-up example shows how the concepts in this book permeate the structure and the people. Three over-arching principles are highlighted; we illustrate how they were demonstrated in the supernatural work.

- The challenges of, and how the Lord works in and through a deliverer/forerunner.
- The interplay of co-dependents, independents and interdependent, and how they were unified so people stayed in their lane to complete the work.

- How the work is aligned with the throne so that the immovable truths are made visible in the people and the structure, thereby attracting favor and resources to the throne of God.

At first glance, one might conclude this work unfolded much like any other work in the natural. However, the deliverer/forerunner role, the supernatural blueprint and throne foundation, allowed the work to overcome obstacles that had thwarted every other previous effort to bring people and resources into a unity of the Spirit, so that a city clean-up of this caliber could be accomplished.

The supernatural equates to GOD DOING IT through human vessels. He is not dependent on our abilities; we are dependent upon his Spirit working in and through us. Therefore, a supernatural work can be a small or large endeavor. What makes it supernatural is that it originated in the heart of God and his Spirit designed the blueprint.

A supernatural work is Spirit-driven and Spirit-led. What that means, in a practical sense, is that as a master builder of a work, the Spirit will guide you in a piecemeal fashion such that you don't recognize in the natural that the steps you are taking are aligning the work with the throne of God. Often, only in retrospect, do we see how the Spirit led us to take certain actions, make specific comments, encourage a co-leader, or move in a new direction that put the work in alignment, or kept the work aligned with God's throne. For this reason, we cannot teach these concepts as a series of steps or actions that will produce a desired result. For every work, only God knows how he will orchestrate it. This is why we must be in-step with the Spirit and his timing.

LOGOS GUIDANCE

As in every supernatural work originated in the heart of God and ordained by his Spirit, the logos Word will be illumined to the deliverer and forerunner(s). This provides the foundation upon which the structure and the people are aligned with the throne, so that favor and resources will be attracted to the work. Every work, without exception, must be aligned with Daniel 7:14 (NKJV), *He was given authority, honor, and sovereignty over all the nations of the world, so that people of every race and nation and language would obey him. His rule is eternal – it will never end. His kingdom will never be destroyed.* In other words, the governing leadership will have both divine authority and designated authority in the natural realm; honor will be evident in the structure and the people; and his kingdom sovereignty will overtake earthly sovereignty and displace it when opposed.

In the following work, all these elements are evident and permeated the structure and the people.

Authority. Authority was evident in the people and structure because the principal deliverer/forerunner (Rose) aligned the work with the throne of God. All the people involved were treated *righteously* (doing the right thing because it was the right thing) and with *justice* (fairness). Authority was delegated based upon people's integrity and work ethic as in Matthew 13:12 (NKJV) *For whoever has, to him more will be given, and he will have abundance; but whoever does not have, even what he has will be taken away from him.* However, all contributors were acknowledged regardless of their level of contribution to the work.

Honor. Everyone involved in the work was affirmed and valued whether young, old or robust. The wisdom of the elderly was honored, particularly in situations in which people were tempted to complain, to bow out of their responsibility or to behave immorally. The robust were honored for their ability to get the work done; while the youth were encouraged to participate as they saw their community working together and the environment improving as a result. They lived what Matthew 25:40 (NKJV) describes, *and the King will answer and say to them, 'Assuredly, I say to you, inasmuch as you did it to one of the least of these My brethren, you did it to Me.'*

Sovereignty. The throne was established within the group; the principles of the throne were visible to the people within the work as a result of authority and honor having been established and recognized by the people. Rose's overarching scriptural principle was Matthew 21:22 (NKJV)—*And whatever things you ask in prayer, believing, you will receive.* She believed God was sovereign over the work and the people. Therefore, it was a matter of asking him for the blueprint and the favor, and then the resources would follow. As the process evolved, the city fathers realized it was coming together. In turn, they granted the leadership a level of authority and support no other group in the city enjoyed.

ROSE'S STORY

The following example provides a practical illustration of the overarching principles outlined above. It demonstrates the challenges and frustrations of deliverer/forerunners; however, these are but necessary labor pains that bring forth the miraculous turnarounds that result when we allow the Spirit to birth the strategy and chart the course.

During a Habitat for Humanity housing project, President Carter visited Benton Harbor, Michigan, to assist with the work. After touring the city, he stated that the city was in a deplorable condition—just plain dirty. The local news media publicized his comments for several weeks. The former President stated, "Even though many of the people living in this city are poor, they certainly do not have to live in dirt and squalor."

I (Rose) had been appointed by the state governor as Executive Director of an organization called Citizens for Progressive Change (CPC). The goal of the organization was to assist local residents with job training, adult education and job placement. As a deliverer/forerunner, the Lord called me to organize block clubs, youth groups, and a working task force that united many of the residents into a cohesive, viable community and resulted in several residents coming to Christ.

After reading the comments of the former President, I resolved to organize the residents and conduct a city wide clean-up. Most said it was an impossible task. Others complained it wasn't worth the effort. However, impressed by the Spirit, I continued to make an appeal to present the city in a clean and wholesome manner, so that visitors could see that we had pride in our environment. Also, the Lord let me know how important it was for the people to have a sense of unity in working and living together. Working together in one spirit for a common goal would not only improve the adult interactions, but would serve as a role model for the youth as well.

I took the idea to the Lord in prayer and fasting. The Holy Spirit responded by giving me a fun approach to organize the residents in the clean-up project. The first instruction was to establish block club members to spread the word about the importance of the clean-up project. I was amazed, although I shouldn't been because I prayed, people began to sign up for the project in record numbers.

A block club is a group of residents who usually live in close proximity that form an organized way to keep watch over their neighborhood and families. Block indicates several blocks of homes, usually 3 to 6, which create a formal setting to conduct business, recreation, and civil obligations. Block clubs allow for self-governing of a small cohesive group that is empowered by their ability to resolve issues and concerns within their association or neighborhoods.

One very successful group was the block club of Agard, Union, May and Jennings Street. A majority of elderly families comprised this group with John Thomas, Sr. serving as president. The Agard, Union, May and Jennings Street club implemented a neighborhood watch program that was adopted throughout the city and other communities as well.

Before the block club started, the neighborhood was in a dreadful condition. Abandoned homes surrounded by tall grass and debris, peppered the neighborhood. Old cars and discarded dishwashers and other appliances cluttered the tenants' yards. Vagrants broke into and lived in the abandoned homes—some were drug users, prostitutes and arsonists who burned some of the abandoned houses. Not surprisingly, with these intruders, the atmosphere in the neighborhood turned violent. The children were not safe and the elderly were afraid to leave their homes. The result was a dismal, crime-ridden environment in which people merely existed day-in and day-out. It was an environment of trepidation, fear and hopelessness.

Challenge to Deliverer/Forerunner

The biggest challenge was myself. A two-week vacation in Benton Harbor turned into residency in the city. My goal was to attend a school of performing arts in Chicago. Instead, God placed me into his school of community re-building. Rather than argue with God, I decided to serve. He had opened this door of opportunity as Executive Director, giving me a position of favor and access to people and resources.

I had some anxiety because I did not have a background in what he had called me to do. On one particular occasion, a prominent community development leader attacked me saying I did not have a background or experience in this area. The Lord used his shepherds, the city pastors, to surround me. They unequivocally informed the community leaders, "If Rose isn't there we won't be there!"

I agonized over not having gotten more education and experience. However, I realized I was trying to rely on my own ability and skills. So I read Proverbs 3:5-6 (NKJV) *Trust in the LORD with all your heart, and lean not on your own understanding; in all your ways acknowledge Him, and*

He shall direct your paths. This passage became a rhema word from the Lord to me. It gave me peace; it was his work not mine. I was merely a vessel. No one had been successful in organizing the different areas of the community to work together. Because of God's favor, we were able to organize the people and recognize them for what they had done, no matter how small the contribution.

The next obstacle was to obtain permission for clean-up from the city fathers. The scripture, "...*Yet you do not have because you do not ask*" (*James 4:2 NKJV*), resonated within me. I approached the city and inquired, "Is there any way to get this done?" They responded with an indisputable NO. "No, we don't have the community development dollars or manpower to do it!" Further, certain authority figures opposed the work because it had not been initiated by them.

When the city said they did not have the money to do it, we (I and the city residents) took it upon ourselves to start the work. At this point, I met John Thomas, a block club president and community activist. John had already established relationships with several city officials because of his community activism. John and I took pictures of the initial completed work and developed a proposal which we presented at a city council meeting. The presentation was so compelling that the city agreed to find support for our project. Within weeks support came from several areas—local business contributions, the Chamber of Commerce, and law enforcement.

As people saw the city beautified, those who had initially opposed the project were now supporters. Despite the people's support, some opposition from officials persisted. Particularly virulent opposition came from the city landlords who did not want to invest money into improving the homes and the environment. They argued that the people would just destroy or neglect the property again. However, the overriding concern was the bottom line—the impact to their pocketbooks.

It became necessary for some residents who had opposing landlords, to seek assistance from the court system. A city ordinance stated landlords were obligated to maintain their property in a manner that was beneficial to the renter and surrounding environment. Many residents utilized this process to obtain the essential resources to make improvements to their home or apartment complex.

Another challenge was the relationship (or lack thereof) between city residents and law enforcement. Prior to the start of the clean-up, residents viewed the police force as an entity designed to harass them. Many of the youth were fearful of police officers because of previous negative interactions. The youth, in particular, viewed law enforcement as the enemy. An open animosity existed between residents and the police force.

The police chief (also a pastor), operating as a forerunner, was aware of residents' perceptions. He decided to rectify the problem. The chief initiated a more approachable and friendly relationship between city residents and law enforcement based upon an innovative strategy. He selected two officers to serve as liaisons between the police department and the residents. Their objective was to provide information and activities to inform residents of the police department's role in protecting the city. For example, the officers made visits to schools, playgrounds and community events. For these visits, they created a robot called Petie. Robot Petie creatively informed his audience of the role and activities of the police department. A typical script of Petie's might sound like, *"Hi, my name is Petie and I roam the halls of the police department each day and I'm here to tell you what they do. Are you interested? I hope you are!* Petie would explain to the audience the daily activities of the police officers, the type of cases they handled and statistics on their successes. He assured the residents that the officers were caring and concerned about the welfare of the community. As a result, people felt freer to ask questions and began to see the role of the law enforcement agency in a better light.

The immediate challenge John (the block president) faced was the lack of equipment and supplies to renovate or clean up the neighborhoods. The city had large equipment such as front-end loaders to take away trees and rubbish. As president, John initiated conversations with the city officials regarding how the city could help with resources and manpower to improve the neighborhoods. The city agreed to supply certain equipment and to waive the fees for trash removal. The city asked the block clubs to create a trash removal schedule. The city also provided surveillance capability. John, and another block club member, were appointed official police liaisons and given the use of a police vehicle to monitor the neighborhoods.

Additionally, community organizations agreed to give block clubs money—Community Dollars. Each block club had to submit an application to receive a $2500 dollar stipend to purchase equipment for neighborhood clean-up.

Three Groups—Seniors, Youth, and Adults

The block club residents comprised three distinct groups. Our challenge was to bring these disparate parties to the table, in a collaborative spirit, to make cleaning up the city a reality. Further, each group contained clusters of co-dependents, independents and interdependent individuals. We saw the potential for combustion amongst these dissimilar groups. To get all parties on the same page, we started weekly informational meetings. This rallied the troops and kept them centered on the purpose. Next, a plan was devised for division of labor. For example, some people cooked for the troops, some people worked with the city, while others performed the actual clean-up.

Seniors. Surprisingly, the seniors, while the oldest and physically the most feeble of the three groups, were both the dominant group and most instrumental in creating the cohesiveness among members necessary to make the block clubs successful. They functioned primarily as *interdependent* members. Seniors aged from 50 to 81 years and were predominantly female. Unique to this group, was that they held fond memories and had formed a strong bond to the neighborhood when it was vibrant and safe. They viewed the block clubs as a vehicle to restablize the neighborhood. These residents had been in the neighborhood the longest and wanted to maintain the pride and strength they felt in their neighborhood before—they wanted that back.

Because of their availability, not employed and primarily present in the neighborhood all hours of the day and night, the seniors became the communications network keeping the other group members informed of schedules, changes, progress, etc. Their primary communication vehicles were the grapevine and the telephone. They maintained contact via telephone and met daily at a senior center. They were the neighborhood watch guards; always at home and able to identify anything abnormal in the environment. Reliability was a strength amongst this group, with even the oldest lady penning a note (that you couldn't read) or calling when she couldn't be present at a meeting.

While a reliable communications network, this group faced a number of challenges. All had fixed incomes which placed them living at or below the poverty level. A large number had health issues. Some lived in substandard housing in unsafe conditions due to lack of resources. Many had no transportation. And a large percentage of seniors had no formal education.

Youth. The youth aged from 14-19. A large percentage of the youth were trouble-makers, rambunctious, with no respect for the community. Some had problems with the court system (petty theft/runaways) and came from one-parent homes. We viewed the young people as a monumental challenge. We would categorize them as *independents* with the primary focus of "doing their own thing." The principal problem appeared to be too much idle time, with no guidance or structure. The youth had not been taught a work ethic, had no respect for authority and lacked positive role models.

To encourage the youths' participation, we offered them small stipends and free meals. This offer appealed to the young people because they had no income to purchase basic necessities that most youth enjoy. As they participated in the work and saw their environment change, they began to exhibit pride in their surroundings. This in turn, stirred them to keep their neighborhood clean rather than litter it.

The seniors were instrumental in dealing with the challenge of the *independent* youth. Some youth continued in deviant, self-serving behavior after committing to the work. To remedy this situation, the seniors spent time coaching the youth regarding responsible conduct. Since many of their parents were young and lacked maturity in their own conduct, the youth had not been exposed to structured behavior. Once the youth began to adhere to the recommendations of the seniors, it produced a good result. They felt calmer, loved, and guided. The positive change in their demeanor affected their interactions with other groups and with each other.

After being mentored by the seniors and adults involved in the clean-up, the youth themselves became role models in the neighborhood. This extended not only to cleanliness but to many other aspects such as not swearing, no loud music and being helpful rather than harmful.

Adults. This group aged 25-42 were the backbone of the work. The group included 45% blue collar workers, 30% disabled; and 25% professionals. The blue collar and professional workers were internet savvy and more mobile because they had transportation. The group readily articulated recommendations and viable solutions to negative issues and circumstances. They were the problem-solvers. Interestingly, they were a mixed group of *co-dependent, independent* and *interdependent individuals.*

Communication was an overriding issue between the groups. The seniors and adults joined forces to rectify the problem. They created communication vehicles and strategies with the seniors focused on telephone communication and the adults the internet. Communications included flyers of special occasions, announcements in the local news media and church bulletins. These served as venues to keep all parties informed. The professional group appealed to businesses and corporations for donations. This group created the fund raising strategies such as bake sales, car washes and community events.

The greatest challenge was to keep the adults invested in the project. Because of work schedules and other commitments, time was a strategic commodity. Additionally, the other groups lacked material assets; therefore, this group was required to provide the bulk of the financial and physical resources to accomplish the mission. Through prayer, God kept the group focused with a mind to work.

Because of the mixture of *co-dependents, independent and interdependent* individuals, several issues arose. Some *independent* individuals decided not to comply with the trash pickup schedule. As a deliverer/forerunner, I informed the adults that anyone in non-compliance would be turned over to law enforcement and issued a ticket. Thus, the consequence of *independent* behavior was either compliance within a specific timeframe, or to pay a heavy fine. A few individuals received tickets, but eventually complied.

Psychological issues arose in response to authority with some *co-dependent* individuals in the adult group. Resistance surfaced when solutions were recommended that did not include the entire group's interaction. However, the reason for this dilemma was the non-participation of the *co-dependents*. They felt they were not knowledgeable enough to contribute. As a forerunner, in these situations, I would call a truce and get everyone in the room and get input from all involved. I recognized the enemy was trying to discourage people with negative thoughts. I addressed the situation through the anointing of the Holy Spirit receiving words of wisdom. In every situation, individuals were freed from their thoughts of insecurity and inadequacy. God empowered the group to move forward.

Aligning the Work with the Throne

To bring all the groups into alignment with the throne, every meeting began with prayer. Prayer brought us into alignment with how the Spirit wanted to guide us through the process. After extended sessions of prayer, the Lord gave me the blueprint of this work. It would be accomplished through *building relationships* between the churches, businesses, and the residents.

A primary avenue of relationship building inspired by the Spirit was *partnership*. The inspiration came through a logos Word: *And if one prevail against him, two shall withstand him; and a threefold cord is not quickly broken*, (Ecclesiastes 4:12 NKJV). Our three-fold cord was comprised of the Spirit, the people with a mission, and those entities willing to partner with us. God assured us this cord would not be broken but would accomplish that for which he had created it.

The Lord led me to approach local churches and businesses to form partnerships in the clean-up. A little known fact of the city is that there are approximately 160 churches in the city of Benton Harbor, which equates to two or more churches per neighborhood. Our goal was not only to partner to get the work done, but to maintain and continue to beautify the city on an ongoing basis.

The layout of the city enhanced our ability to form partnerships because nearly all of the neighborhood block clubs were clustered around established churches. I appealed to the pastors of these neighborhood churches to form partnerships with the block club in their vicinity. The partnership objective was to form communication networks, resource pools, and neighborhood watch programs. After much discussion, meetings and collaborative effort, everyone agreed that the crime, the vice and disruption had to change. As a result, the idea of relationship building became a reality. The three-fold cord example was adopted and many of those relationships exist to this day.

Despite our eventual success, we encountered opposition in aligning our project with God's throne. In one segment of the city, a closed-membership ministers' alliance existed. This group felt we were imposing upon them. Their position was that correction of the vice and prostitution in the city was a matter for the police, not the church. The ministers expressed grave concern about retribution from the criminal community. When I became aware of this mindset, I gathered a group of residents and business owners. We held a meeting with the concerned churches.

Over the course of several meetings, many residents voiced their concerns that the churches should be more visible and interactive in the affairs of the neighborhood. They emphasized, that according to the Word of God, believers were supposed to be the light and salt of the earth. How could they exemplify light and salt without taking part in neighborhood issues? Several of the influential pastors held a private meeting. The outcome was that the pastors determined the residents' position had merit. These pastors began recruiting other churches and successfully brought most of the churches onboard to assist in the transformation of the city.

In another instance, after several sessions of prayer and fasting, a number of the pastors and block club leaders met with key drug lords to share the vision of cleaning up the city. To the surprise of everyone at the meetings, the drug lords agreed that the city needed a *face lift*. While the drug lords did not commit to total abandonment of their criminal activity, they did agree to curtail their interaction with the youth. They also committed to police abandoned homes, so that no one could gain occupancy and disrupt the neighborhoods by turning them into crack houses. Within a six-month timeframe, many of the drug-ridden, abandoned houses were vacated. This was indicative of another successful aspect of the city-wide clean-up—God was on the move!

Within the context of the groups, God made visible his immovable truths. The love of God became a compelling force. People began to learn about each other, respect each other and work together for a common goal. Like Nehemiah, they began to build a *wall of protection* around their neighborhoods. Although the clean-up project experienced ongoing opposition, the people struggled as a unified group to accomplish a mission that critics had deemed impossible.

One example of God's love at work involved children-at-risk. During the course of the clean-up, workers found children-at-risk—children whose parents were not at home because they were working or drug addicts. In these homes, the older child was responsible to take care of siblings. When work group members encountered these situations, they appealed to the churches for clothing; they appealed to businesses for funds and to supermarkets and food banks for food. Further, they scheduled meetings with the parents of these homes. They encouraged them to seek counseling and drug rehabilitation services. Several of the churches played a key role in assisting the parents in this process. They transported parents and children on an ongoing basis to needed services.

Additionally, God made visible his justice through his love. The law enforcement community liaisons assigned to the neighborhoods appealed to the court system to allow the neighborhood first-time, young offenders to be mentored rather than charged with an offense. The two police officers took the six youths under their wing. They formed a basketball league. During the clean-ups, the officers permitted the youth to ride in the squad car throughout the community. They introduced the youth to the community arts association and other meaningful recreational activities. These actions helped to reinforce the positive interaction between law enforcement and the youth, and the community as a whole.

Upon completion of clean-up project, former President Carter returned to the city to assist with building twenty-three new homes to be purchased by first time home owners. In his departing speech, he and his wife, Rosalynn, complimented the city saying they were pleased to have been part of such a gratifying experience. He was amazed at how agreeable the entire city looked—much cleaner, with a number of positive transformation dynamics in place. He praised the residents and the work—we praised God for his faithfulness and the culmination of aligning the work with the throne. What a mighty God we serve!

PRACTICING THE CONCEPTS IN THIS BOOK

As this book was in the final stages of the editing process, Rose and I began to experience conflict. At first we were both taken aback. Despite our opposite temperaments, and that we process and act on information differently, we had functioned in unity of the Spirit throughout the revelatory process and the actual writing. However, when we moved into the publishing and distribution stage, conflict erupted. Truthfully, it was a friend who had edited our book, who confronted the situation saying, "You are not doing what the book says!"

There are times when the Lord has to hit you between the eyes with your own revelation. This was one of them. Graciously, our friend set up a meeting with us at a local deli-cafe. This session followed the protocol outlined in this book of *getting everyone in the room* for a discussion and documenting the feedback (Chapter 9, under the sub-heading *Light to Guide the Nations*).

I arrived with our manuscript in hand. Rose and I sat on the couch and our friend sat directly across from us. We began our session with prayer asking the Holy Spirit to guide us. We prayed in the Spirit taking over the atmosphere to expose the works of the enemy. Our friend took the manuscript and opened it to the third chapter—*Called to Unity*. She started the conversation by stating, "I love you both and I know this book is God's revelation." She told us how God had radically changed her as she read it. Then she stated matter-of-factly, "We are going to identify the root problem using the process outlined in this book."

Rose and I briefly gave a synopsis of our disagreement which centered on the content of the *Promotion and Distribution* section of our book proposal and a website under construction. In regard to the Promotion and Distribution content and the conflict it generated, we had met earlier in the week. The conflict around this topic was the genesis of our discovering we had departed from God's blueprint; we were attempting to fit this supernatural work into a structure of the world by submitting the book to a traditional publisher. God had not told us to submit this book proposal. We came to this decision through the advice of another Christian author, which *seemed reasonable* at the time. We had almost fallen prey to one of the greatest pitfalls of a supernatural work, aligning it with the pattern of the world rather than allowing God to reveal the publishing pattern!

After listening to our areas of disagreement, our friend looked us directly in the eye, and stated, "You are each operating as an *independent* which has opened the door to a spirit of rebellion."

We arrived at a decision point, either to humble ourselves and receive the correction, or to continue on a path that had opened a door to a spirit of rebellion. Proverbs 10:17(AMP) is clear on this point, *He who heeds instruction and correction is [not only himself] in the way of life [but also] is a way of life for others. And he who neglects or refuses reproof [not only himself] goes astray [but also] causes to err and is a path toward ruin for others.* It was apparent that God was intervening to bring counsel through our friend. *The godly give good advice to their friends; the wicked lead them astray* (Proverbs 12:26 NLT).

We walked through the protocol outlined in Chapter 3, beginning with casting out the spirit of rebellion and the co-habiting spirits; and secondly, submitting our wills to the rule and authority of Christ. Both Rose and I confessed our sin and asked forgiveness of the other. We discussed our areas of difference, stating our feelings and the reasoning behind our actions. We realized we had both made inaccurate assumptions based on email communications. We had formed perceptions of the other's actions, based on those assumptions, and they were inaccurate as well.

The next day, I captured the *learnings* from this session (see outline below). They included: 1) adhering to God's approach and attitude in accomplishing a supernatural work; 2) creating processes to facilitate understanding so that we are not operating out of false assumptions and perceptions; 3) developing a definitive outline of confrontation in a Culture of Honor. Ensuring we start from the foundational premise — each individual is a child of the King; clearly articulating our purpose, goal and objective, as well as how to manifest the root problem; and 4) the accountabilities and responsibilities of each party when co-laboring on an assignment.

Learnings

- We are working in light of *eternity* not *time*. God is not in a *hurry*. When we feel *pressured* into a decision, or make snap decisions (outside of crisis situations), we are allowing the enemy access to infiltrate.

- God is as concerned about *how* we do a work for him as he is in our completing the assignment.

- We must be willing to <u>check our perceptions</u> with the other person(s), *not pray* about it assuming our perceptions are accurate.

- Confrontation from a **Culture of Honor**[1] perspective, allows God's glory in that individual to arise, as we are operating from the premise that each individual is royalty — a child of the King. They are to be valued for *who they are* not what they bring to the table.
    - Our **purpose** is to identify the "root problem" not to attack or apportion blame
    - Our **goal** is to surface what is hindering the gifts and anointing in that person/persons from operating in unity and at full potential. The **objective** is to fully value and maximize each individual's contribution.

- We must come to the table with the understanding that *each party contributed to the problem*. There is no "innocent" party. Our behavior, understanding, attitude, motive, and/or position are all suspect—they are on the operating table for the Holy Spirit to dissect.
  - For the root problem to *manifest*, each individual is willing:
    - To check our pride at the door and humble ourselves under the scalpel of the Holy Spirit's scrutiny
    - To honor and value the individual(s)
    - To trust the process
    - To be transparent

> In co-laboring, we don't come to the table with solutions but options. This means we do our *due diligence* and research options, outlining the pros and cons of each option. In discussion, a solution will *emerge*. It may be one of the options or an entirely unique solution that evolved out of the discussion. This is how we access the revelatory realm because we are not being confined to our own thought processes.

> When an assignment is produced that does not meet the guidelines, our expectations or standards, *both parties* must assume responsibility to identify the problem.
- The *assigner* must ask him or herself:
  - Were my instructions clear?
  - Did I provide an appropriate example or visual for clarity?
  - Where applicable, did I give the person freedom to choose an alternative method or process to complete the assignment?
  - Did I allow sufficient time and provide the necessary resources for the assignee to complete the assignment with excellence?

- The *assignee* must ask him or herself:
  - Did I understand the expectations?
  - Did I allow myself sufficient time to complete the assignment to the level of the expectation?
  - Did I seek clarity from the assigner on anything that was not clear?
  - Did I fully engage my talents and resources to produce an excellent outcome?

I'd like to report that all conflict was resolved in this one instance. But, as we are human, that was not the case. Opportunities arise for conflict in every supernatural work and they must be dealt with on an ongoing basis.

The scripture alerts us that we must watch as well as pray. *Watch and pray, lest you enter into temptation. The spirit indeed is willing, but the flesh is weak* (Matthew 26:41 NKJV). Nehemiah, and those rebuilding the wall, dealt with enemies daily. External enemies tried to thwart their progress through demonically-inspired intimidation and accusation. Internally, they had to face themselves; their own failures and flaws which resulted in conflicts and rivalries.

The builders worked with a tool in one hand and a warring instrument in the other. Sometimes, the war is internal and the tool is a *threshing* instrument. God is taking us through the fire, breaking us of pride, self-will, and confidence in our own abilities. At other times, we face spiritual wickedness in high places (Eph. 6:12). The war is external. We wield our *warring* instrument— the Sword of the Spirit (Eph. 6:17). Entering into the high praises of God, we war in the Spirit with his Word. The saving grace is the battle is not ours, it "*...is the Lord's*" (I Samuel 17:47 NKJV).

Nonetheless, we must continually remind ourselves that we have a God assignment. This changes our perspective from self to God. We resolve our differences because he birthed this supernatural work in our heart. He revealed the blueprint; it was ordained by him and it is for his glory. Thus, we stay in our lane, despite a few detours and minor crashes on the Highway of Holiness. We keep our eyes focused in the direction of our eternal reward—longing for those precious words from his lips, "*Well done, good and faithful servant; you were faithful over a few things, I will make you ruler over many things. Enter into the joy of your lord*" (Matthew 25:21 NKJV).

GLOSSARY OF TERMS

Anointing. The anointing is the power and presence of God manifested in a committed vessel yielded to the Holy Spirit. (*Examples*: David—1 Samuel 16; Elijah—1 Kings 18; Paul—Acts 13; Peter—Acts 3.)

Atmosphere. An atmosphere is a surrounding influence or environment. An atmosphere can be Holy Spirit influenced or demonically influenced. It is the believer's responsibility to appropriate his/her God-given authority to influence an environment through prayer and supplication. The believer is to charge an atmosphere with God's presence through declaration, decree and agreement with the Word of God. A Spirit-filled believer has the authority to change the atmosphere by casting out the demonic presence permeating a specific atmosphere. (*Example*: Slave girl possessed with a spirit of divination that was demonically speaking into the atmosphere following Paul as he ministered in Philippi—Acts 16:16-19). Believers also intercede permeating the atmosphere with God's Word and requesting his divine intervention of deliverance and protection. (*Example*: The church in Jerusalem warring in prayer for Peter in prison and God sending his angel to supernaturally release Peter—Acts

12:5-11). Or, in displacing principalities, to war in the Spirit, in which God sends out the heavenly host to take the territory in the second heaven, unseating the demonic ruler. (*Example*: The prayer and supplication of Daniel resulted in God sending Michael to war with the spiritual ruler of Persia in the second heaven in answer to Daniel's words which were *heard*—Daniel 10:11-13.)

Breaker Anointing. A breaker anointing is the power and presence of God operating through an individual who overcomes demonic opposition through God pulling down strongholds of the enemy in the spiritual realm, prior to physically taking the territory. (*Example:* David inquired of the Lord whether to attack the Philistines and the Lord broke through before David [..."*The LORD has broken through my enemies before me, like a breakthrough of water."* 2 Sam. 5:20 NKJV] so he could conquer the enemy at Baal Perazim—2 Samuel 5:17-25). The Psalms offer many examples of David overcoming demonic opposition in prayer and commanding his soul to be steadfast in the Lord before going out to fight a battle (Psalm 7; Psalm 13; Psalm 17; Psalm 18).

Celestial Truths. Celestial truths are biblical commands such as our commandment to love one another (John 13:34). They are represented in the 10 commandments that guide our relationship with God and our fellow man. Celestial truths are founded upon immovable and immutable laws and principles that govern the Kingdom of God. For example, the *principle of reciprocity* is an immutable law of *judging* in the kingdom. The measure of your condemnation or forgiveness of others will be the same measurement used to judge you. It is no respecter of persons; it states, *Give, and it shall be given unto you; good measure, pressed down, and shaken together, and running over, shall men give into your bosom. For with the same measure that ye mete withal it shall be measured to you again* (Luke 6:38 KJV). Celestial truths also represent God established patterns and protocols such as God's pattern and protocol for worship. The pattern is that we worship him in Spirit and in Truth (John 4:24); the protocol is: 1) that we enter through the gates of thanksgiving; 2) progress through the outer court of cleansing: 3) enter into the inner court of praise; and 4) move into the holy place of complete surrender to, and adoration of, the King (following the pattern of the Temple—Psalm 100:4).

Charismatic Witchcraft. Charismatic witchcraft is a counterfeit spirit rooted in human charisma. It is a counterfeit authority that operates through manipulation, control and man-pleasing influences that displace the Holy Spirit. This counterfeit spirit can be discerned whenever motives are driven by domination, manipulation, intimidation and emotional blackmail. (*Examples:* Jezebel—I Kings 19 & 21; Simon the Sorcerer—Acts 8:9-24.)

Co-dependent. Individuals who are co-dependent function as though they have no capacity of their own. They communicate in a manner that speaks to others *"I have nothing of value to give"* Consequently, they look to others as their source. Intellectually, they understand they are unique and no one can contribute what they alone have to offer—unfortunately, they do not believe it in their spirit. They tend to be unbalanced to one extreme or the other on a *contributor/receiver* continuum. (*Example:* Hagar describes this type of individual, who, as a slave, was demure and submissive to her masters; however, when her circumstances changed—she became pregnant with Abram's child, she swung to the opposite end of the continuum and became a "taker" mocking her mistress. She did not take responsibility for her actions but blamed Sarah. She perceived her value in her ability to conceive, not in being a unique creation of God—Genesis 16:1-9.)

Co-laborer. A co-laborer is a vital contributor in a supernatural work that is founded on God's governmental structure, and functions by anointed, delegated authority from God's throne. A co-laborer operates in an environment that is non-hierarchical and that seeks to support, value and honor the contributions of all its members. (*Example*: The priests and the men of the city worked together to rebuild the walls with half taking responsibility for specific portions of the wall while the other half stood guard for protection—Nehemiah 3 & 4.)

Deacons/Co-laboring leaders. Deacons represent the administrative, hands-on, delegated authority of the work. As they have internalized the vision, they function as practical movers—carrying the mission to completion. They function to keep the work on-track and enforce the governmental authority of the elders. They operate with authority over specific areas of the work. Deacons collaborate with governing leaders and co-laborers to keep the work in alignment and progressing toward the goal. (*Example*: the seven men chosen to administer the feeding program in the church at Jerusalem—Acts 6:1-6.)

Deliverer. A deliverer is God's chosen instrument to establish righteousness and justice. (In speaking of David, who delivered Israel from all her enemies by the hand of the Lord, the Queen of Sheba declared,

"Blessed be the Lord your God, who delighted in you, setting you on the throne of Israel! Because the Lord has loved Israel forever, therefore He made you king, to do justice and righteousness." I Kings 10:9 NKJV.) The Lord sets his mantle of kingdom authority upon this individual, to align all aspects of the supernatural work with his throne. The deliverer is charged to make visible God's celestial truths in the people and the structure. Historically, biblical deliverers have been born into a hostile environment. Moses, Joseph, Elijah, and Jesus are a few examples of deliverers. The deliverer learns to live in the constant dichotomy of favor and hostility and rise above it. The Lord anoints the deliverer as a catalyst of transformation in the earth.

Destiny. Destiny is the pre-designed course God has created for our life from the foundation of the world. (*Examples:* Jeremiah' call to be a prophet to the nations—Jeremiah 1:5; Paul's Damascus road experience—Acts 26:12-18.)

Dunamis (power). *Dunamis* is a Greek word which means miraculous power and ability. It is a power that transcends our natural abilities and supernaturally transforms physical, emotional, and intellectual states. It is the creative essence of God manifested through a human vessel. The dunamis is the *resurrection power* that raised Christ from the dead (Rom. 1:4; Phil. 3:10). There is no comparable power in the earthly realm that brings to life that which was dead, and creates into being that which was not (Rom. 4:17)!

Elders/co-leaders/governing leaders. Elders are the spiritual undergirding and function to build the foundation of a supernatural work. They have authority and accountability over *all* areas of the work. The elders' main objective is to create an environment that imparts unity of the Spirit, so that work and the people operate in one accord with the mind of Christ. (*Example*: the apostles—Acts 6.) They function to guide and assist others in internalizing the vision. Requirements to function as an elder include: maturity in the faith; the anointing of the seven-fold Holy Spirit and evidence of spiritual fruit that remains.

Forerunner. A forerunner is an individual who has received God's vision. He or she is obedient to the voice of the Lord, following the leadings of the Holy Spirit. A forerunner breaks through into new territory in the spirit with God, and then sets a course for others to follow. (*Examples:* John the Baptist prepared the way for the Messiah; through his preaching of repentance, he set believers on the course leading to the New

Covenant (Mark 1:4; Acts19:4). The apostle Paul experienced a number of revelations and heavenly visitations that prepared him to breakthrough both spiritually and in the natural, to expand the gospel into new territory, that of the gentiles—2 Cor. 12:1-7.) A forerunner restores lost truths and unveils "truths" to the body. God chose Paul, a former Pharisee and scholar of the Old Testament Scriptures, to unveil the truth to the church that they had been chosen to be in the Messiah before the foundation of the world—Eph. 1:4.) In our present church age, the Bible is complete and the unveiled truths are a deeper, revelatory understanding of the text. A forerunner restores lost truths to the Body of Christ such as the true meaning of biblical repentance. A forerunner is the instrument through which God reveals the pattern of the supernatural work and the blueprints for building it. (*Example:* Nehemiah prayed and God gave him detailed plans for his journey to Jerusalem and rebuilding the walls—Nehemiah 1 & 2.) The Lord imparts a breaker anointing upon a forerunner. This anointing breaks demonic opposition to restore what was lost and brings to Earth the new thing that God is doing.

Governing leaders. Governing leaders are governmental leaders (Deliverer, Forerunner, Elder) in the kingdom whose role is to establish the celestial truths of God's throne (i.e., biblical commands and principles) making them evident in the work structure and the people.

Government of God Structure. The government of God is a structure that is founded on righteousness and justice, the pillars of God's throne (Psalm 97:2). The structure functions by anointed, delegated authority from that throne. It is non-hierarchical in nature and seeks to support, value and honor the contributions of all its members (1 Cor. 12).

Independent. Independent individuals view contribution, participation and aspects of their role in terms of personal impact. They tend to operate from a position of how circumstances and people personally affect them. Independents seek experiential knowledge and revelation knowledge but keep it to themselves neglecting to fellowship and share their experiences and knowledge with others. They are taking everything in, but not giving out or connecting with the body of Christ. This mode of operation is based on a *self-serving* model not the servant model of the kingdom. (*Examples*: The most infamous independent was the disciple Judas Iscariot who betrayed Jesus—John 12:4; John 18:2. Another biblical independent was King Saul who sought his own way and the honor of man over obedience to God—1 Samuel 15.)

Interdependent. Interdependent individuals operate through mutual exchange—in two-way relationships. They view themselves as part of a whole and desire to contribute their portion while supporting the contributions of others. This frees every individual to fulfill their assignment in the supernatural work. Interdependence promotes trust, as it allows for dissension without destroying the bond of unity. An interdependent individual's source of sustaining power is Christ. Interdependents allow Christ to work through them, embodying the vision and the divine purpose. (*Example:* The apostle Paul is the most illustrative model of an interdependent in the New Testament—Acts 15:1-24; Rom. 9:1-3; 12:1-11; 1 Cor. 1:10-13; Col. 1:24-29; 1 Tim. 4 & 5; Gal. 4:15, 6:1-10.)

Mantle. A mantle is a measure of authority, stature and God-given ability, including spiritual gifts, to fulfill the mission of an individual's calling. The mantle God places upon a person will be recognized by others. Those designated to be a part of the work will be attracted to the individual's mantle and submit to the governmental anointing of the mantle. A mantle stays with a mission and is transferable to another God-designated leader. (*Examples:* Elijah physically and spiritually placed his mantle upon Elisha—1 Kings 19:19. Moses placed a portion of his spiritual mantle upon Joshua through the laying on of hands—Num. 27:15-21.)

Master Builder. A master builder is a governing leader (deliverer, forerunner, elder), whose leadership flows out of the principles of God's Word and is guided by the moment-by-moment instruction of the Holy Spirit. Guided by the light of his presence and Word, a master builder builds according to the pattern of the kingdom. He or she will not deviate from the blueprint God has revealed for the supernatural work. A master builder ensures righteousness and justice permeate the building process by adhering to a kingdom structure and principles in accomplishing the work. (*Examples:* The apostles were master builders building the church upon the foundation of Jesus Christ—Matthew 16:13-20; Paul was a master builder among the gentiles and laid the scriptural foundation of the majority of the New Testament through his letters to the various churches—1 Cor. 3:9-15; Nehemiah is a primary example of a master builder charged with both a physical rebuilding of the Temple and the spiritual rebuilding of the people—Book of Nehemiah).

Mission. The mission is the specific supernatural work for which God has revealed the blueprint and called us to accomplish in the earth. (*Examples*: Paul—Gal. 1:11-15; Jesus—Luke 4:16-21.)

Glossary Of Terms

Supernatural Work. A supernatural work is one in which God is the author and builder of the framework. God reveals the pattern and structure and the work is accomplished through a deliverer/forerunner and God's chosen co-laborers. (*Examples:* Moses receives the blueprint for the Tabernacle in the wilderness—Exodus 25:8-10; Jesus reveals the New Testament worship pattern (in Spirit and Truth)—John 4:23.)

Unity of the Spirit. Unity of the Spirit signifies a state of *oneness* with the Godhead and the heavenly realm; we are restored to our rightful authority of dominion in the earth (Luke 9:1; Luke 10:9). Our oneness (unity) in the spiritual realm has seated us in heavenly places with Christ Jesus. *And hath raised us up together, and made us sit together in heavenly places in Christ Jesus* (Ephesians 2:6 KJV). From our heavenly location, we have access to God's throne. Here God reveals heavenly strategy—the purposes of his heart for the divine work he has called us to perform. Unity of the Spirit is the precursor to the manifestation of God's glory (2 Chron. 5:13) in which healing, miracles, signs and wonders are instantaneous (Acts 5:15).

Vision. The "eyes" of our faith's destination is internal carrying us to a person, Christ. A vision is emergent and manifests when we come into unity of the Spirit, which releases the power and anointing to fulfill the work. Hab. 2:3 KJV—*For the vision is yet for an appointed time; but at the end it will speak, and it will not lie. Though it tarries, wait for it; because it will surely come, it will not tarry.*

Warfare Worship. This form of worship requires the worshipper to assume the position of warrior. Our warrior is the Lord—*The LORD is a warrior; Yahweh is his name* (Exodus 15:3 NLT). In warfare worship, the Lord goes before us to offensively engage the enemy, tearing down his strongholds in the second heaven. Initially, we enter in through thanksgiving and the high praises of God. We seek God's heart and counsel and then do the word that has been revealed.

END NOTES

Chapter 1

1. Signet Ring. *God's signet ring*. Retrieved April 22, 2011. *http://gracethrufaith.com/ask-a-bible-teacher/gods-signet-ring/*.

2. Zerubbabel—Hebrew *zarab (2215)* & *babel (894)*. In *Strongs Exhaustive Concordance online*. Retrieved April 22, 2011. *http://www.biblestudytools.com/lexicons/hebrew/kjv/zerubbabel.html*.

3. Connell, K. (2012). *Normalizing evil*. Houghton, MI: Extended Life Training Center, Inc., 15.

4. Mc Clean, R. (2005). *Eternity invading time*. Altamonte Springs, FL: Advantage Books.

5. Definition of substance. *Encarta World English Dictionary online (North American Ed.)* & (P) 2009 Microsoft Corporation.

6. Definition of evidence. Ibid.

7. Greek *Pistis* (4102). Strong, J. (1996). In *The new strongs exhaustive concordance* Nashville, TN: Thomas Nelson Publishers, (71, Greek).

Chapter 2

1. Definition of Humility. Jesus is our model of humility concept. Retrieved May 18, 2011. *http://www.voiceofonecrying.com/humility.html*.

Chapter 4

1. Hebrew *Miqdash* (4720).In *The new strongs exhaustive concordance* Nashville, TN: Thomas Nelson Publishers, (84, Hebrew).

2. Hebrew *Dabar* (1696). In *The new strongs exhaustive concordance* Nashville, TN: Thomas Nelson Publishers, (30, Hebrew).

3. Charismatic Witchcraft. *Charismatic Witchcraft*. Retrieved June, 1, 2011. *http://www.tpwmi.com/charismaticwitchcraft.html*.

Chapter 5

1. R. Phillips (2010). *Everyone's guide to demons & spiritual warfare*. Lake Mary, FL: Charisma House, 148.

2. G. Keller (2004). *Father: A search into the heart of God*. Fort Mill, SC: Morning Star Publications, 182-183.

Chapter 7

1. Iniquity. *Webster's new world dictionary of the american language*. David B. Guralnik (2nd College Ed.) (1968). Wm. Collins + World Publishing Co, Inc. Cleveland, 725.

2. Rejection. Ibid. p. 1198.

3. Bevere, J. (1993). *The voice of one crying*. Apopka, FL: Messenger Press, 79-93.

Chapter 8

1. Howell, D. N. (2003). *Servants of the servant: A biblical theology of leadership.* Eugene, OR: Wipf & Stock Publishers, 3.

2. Ibid. p. 3.

3. Ibid. p. 219.

4. Hebrew *Chayil* (2428). Strong, J. (1996). In *The new strongs exhaustive concordance* Nashville, TN: Thomas Nelson Publishers, (42, Hebrew).

5. Howell, D. N. (2003). *Servants of the servant: A biblical theology of leadership.* Eugene, OR: Wipf & Stock Publishers, 1.

6. Ibid. p. 160.

Chapter 9

1. Johnson, B. (2011, August). *Honoring the fathers and mothers.* Presented at the Jesus Culture Awakening, Chicago, IL.

2. Silk, D. (2009). *Culture of honor: Sustaining a supernatural environment.* Shippensburg, PA: Destiny Image Publishers, Inc., 29.

3. Synonyms of diverse. *Merriam Webster Dictionary online.* Retrieved September 8, 2011. http://www.merriam-webster.com/dictionary/diverse.

Chapter 11

1. Definition of atmosphere. *Merriam Webster Dictionary online.* Retrieved September 9, 2011. http://www.merriam-webster.com/dictionary/atmosphere.

2. Greek *plana*☐ (4105). Strong, J. (1996). In *The new strongs exhaustive concordance* Nashville, TN: Thomas Nelson Publishers, (71, Greek).

3. Johnson, B. (2007). *Face to face with God.* Lake Mary, FL: Charisma House Publishers, 53.

Epilogue—Concepts in Practice

1. Silk, D. (2009). *Culture of honor: Sustaining a supernatural environment.* Shippensburg, PA: Destiny Image Publishers, Inc., 34.

Made in the USA
Charleston, SC
08 March 2013